MW00905024

# Whisky Today© 2006

## Michael Gill

Note for Librarians: A cataloguing record for this book is available from Library and Archives Canada at www.collectionscanada.ca/amicus/index-e.html
ISBN 1-4120-8328-1

*Printed in Victoria, BC, Canada. Printed on paper with minimum 30% recycled fibre. Trafford's print shop runs on "green energy" from solar, wind and other environmentally-friendly power sources.*

PUBLISHING™

*Offices in Canada, USA, Ireland and UK*
This book was published *on-demand* in cooperation with Trafford Publishing. On-demand publishing is a unique process and service of making a book available for retail sale to the public taking advantage of on-demand manufacturing and Internet marketing. On-demand publishing includes promotions, retail sales, manufacturing, order fulfilment, accounting and collecting royalties on behalf of the author.

**Book sales for North America and international:**
Trafford Publishing, 6E–2333 Government St.,
Victoria, BC  V8T 4P4  CANADA
phone 250 383 6864 (toll-free 1 888 232 4444)
fax 250 383 6804; email to orders@trafford.com
**Book sales in Europe:**
Trafford Publishing (UK) Limited, 9 Park End Street, 2nd Floor
Oxford, UK  OX1 1HH  UNITED KINGDOM
phone 44 (0)1865 722 113 (local rate 0845 230 9601)
facsimile 44 (0)1865 722 868; info.uk@trafford.com
**Order online at:**
trafford.com/06-0083

10  9  8  7  6  5  4  3  2

# Message from the Author

Selling alcoholic beverages for over 25 years, has given me the opportunity to sample and enjoy many fine wines, ales, ports and of course single malts. Growing up in England and working in various parts of the world, I have had the good fortune to meet an incredible range of people in the industry along with friends and customers that share my passion for single malts.

The beverage industry is one of the most competitive industries in the world and requires hard work and dedication in order to succeed. Selling is one thing; however public speaking, teaching classes and writing articles were talents that I had once thought were beyond my simple life.

All that changed when I began to represent single malt distilleries and had the opportunity to spend time with Bruichladdich, Isle of Arran and Cooley's just to name a few. The more I promote this mysterious golden nectar, the more I want to educate the growing legions of single malt drinkers.

I now have the whisky bug and spend of all my spare time studying single malts along with the other Scottish past time, golf. I trust this book will take out some the confusion, dispel the myths, and make your shopping experience even better. (See Table "A" for our Savvy Shopping Guide)

Michael J. Gill

*Apologies for any errors or omissions which will be corrected in future additions of this book.*

*Please email any comments to the author - michael.gill@superiorbeverages.ca*

Dedication

To my Mum & Dad

You have always been there for me

through thick and thin!

# Acknowledgements

*I would like to thank my "A" Team for their marvelous support through 2005. Janet Couper & Miriam Beach of Schooner Cove Gallery (Graphics) Meredith White and Leah Gough (Editing).*

*Special thanks go to Peter Conn, Chief Editor of Boom Magazine for the opportunity to write my whisky column.*

*Mostly, I want to thank my wife, Debra for all her support and hours helping me put this book together. Whisky Today would not have been possible to write without the outstanding support of, Debra. She is my backup quarterback in all aspects of my life including running our business and the formatting, design and collation of this book. While Debra is not a NFL Football fan, I have explained numerous times, that Tom Brady (the back up quarterback in 2001–2002 Season) led the New England Patriots to the Superbowl and won! The biggest compliment an avid sports fan could bestow on their partner.*

# About the Author

*Michael Gill has spent the past twenty years in the beverage industry in a sales and marketing management capacity. Presently, the owner of a beverage agency, Michael represents many fine single malt distilleries and wineries from all over the world. He teaches single malt appreciation classes and writes a quarterly column in Boom Magazine. Michael resides in Atlantic Canada with his wife Debra, three cats and a dog.*

*Cover Photograph by Michael Gill, March 29, 2004 "Isle of Arran Sunset."*

# Table of Contents

# Introduction

*"Single malts aren't for talking lad, they're for supping" said Uncle Peter – a typical Yorkshire man!*

He does have a point on the supping that single malt whiskies are the easiest alcohol beverage to enjoy however, they are certainly the most complicated beverage to understand. In my more recent experience, the whisky industry has piqued the interest of consumers who are now seeking more knowledge about this unique beverage.

There are thousands of web sites and numerous books on whisky so why read this one? I have worked in the alcoholic beverage industry for 25 years and have sold whisky for quite some time. I have yet to see a whisky book written by a sales professional who sells whisky for a living to retail shops, restaurants and pubs. Being in the trenches (so to speak) in one of the most competitive industries in the world requires one to have extensive product knowledge and special sales and marketing skills to be successful. This book is unique in its writing style and content; and I hope my experience and observations will be interesting and useful when shopping for your next single malt whisky.

Single malt whisky is the most mysterious and debated alcoholic beverage in the world. The industry has been like the secret service with an "us" and "them" attitude – you enjoy drinking it, we will keep making it. Scotland produces whisky in a way that mirrors their country, beautiful and unique, with an aura that is both magical and mysterious. However, today's society is inquisitive and demands to know more about its lifestyle products.

In the last twenty years drinking habits have moved away from the regular trip to the pub to discuss topics such as politics, the weather and sports. Today we drink more than 80% of our favorite tipples at home, often with friends over dinner. Wine, port and single malts play an important part in our dialogue, and the hosts demand information concerning what they are serving their guests.

Also, the information contained within this guide is up to date, and through modern technology will continue to be updated each year. Through my own fault, I purchased a whisky book in 2004 that I thought was "new." After I purchased it, I discovered that is was a reprint from 1997! By the time I realized this, I was halfway across the Atlantic heading home and couldn't very well return it – oh well, it was time to put on the headphones and watch the in-flight movie! There are so many changes in this industry every year never mind seven!

The numerous guides on nosing, tastings and scores are fine for the connoisseurs who believe they understand a particular single malt that may have aromas of coconut and mangos with tastes of lemon meringue pie, chocolate éclairs and bubble gum. I really do not believe that the ordinary consumer who enjoys a good dram would ever pick up these subtle nuances.

My desire is to take you on a journey in whisky, dispel the myths and take out the confusion in buying whisky so that it can be more unpretentious and fun. This book will give you a complete understanding of single malt whisky, the latest news and trends in the industry and a better shopping experience. The matching of whisky with cheese is cutting edge (so to speak) and will be very popular in years to come. I hope my readers will be the first pioneers in this gastronomic delight.

Enjoy – Slainthe

**Chapter**

# 1

# Whisky Industry Today

Why is whisky a big deal today? Why all the changes in an art that spans back hundreds of years? Have the facts changed that much from 100 years ago?

Yup, the single malt industry has changed dramatically in the last decade! There are only approximately 85 distilleries left in Scotland today. The actual number of distilleries originally in production seems to be a bit of a mystery. There were at least 200 distilleries alive and well at the beginning of the 19th century. From that point onwards, there has been a steady decline and in the 1980's at least 30 distilleries were mothballed or closed down permanently. (See Table "C")

In the last decade, a further 25 or so working distilleries were either also mothballed or closed. In the summer of 2005, Pernod Ricard along with Fortune Brands bought Allied Domecq. These made Pernod Ricard, along with Diageo, the two largest owners of Scottish distilleries and now represent over half of the distilleries in Scotland – thus, the reference to David and Goliath in the above drawing. The David's represent the smaller, independently run whisky distilleries and the major players are represented by Goliath.

*Before I delve into "Whisky Today," it is important to understand how all this started!*

Whisky has been one of the most popular drinks for hundreds of years both medicinally and for pleasure. There were several factors in the 19th and 20th centuries that pushed whisky sales higher, even with the dreaded taxman's hold on whisky production in Scotland.

Firstly, scotch became more popular to a wider market in the 1830s with the invention of the Patent/Coffey Still known today as the Continuous Still. This invention led to large scale production of grain whisky and an increase in popularity of Scotch whisky as a result. These stills produced whisky much more efficiently than the traditional pot stills, but with much less flavour. Quickly, merchants began blending the malt whisky with the grain whisky distilled in the continuous stills, making the first blended Scotch whisky. Such producers as Chivas and Johnny Walker jumped on the bandwagon and were an immediate success not only in the United Kingdom but throughout the world.

From 1830 onwards blended Scotch proved to be a hot commodity. It was less expensive to produce than single malts; however, the addition of malt gave the product more flavour and character than grain alone. The combination of malt and grain allowed the distilleries to produce larger quantities of single malts to be used in the blended whisky industry.

Secondly, in 1870 vineyards of France were devastated by the phylloxera beetle plague. Within a few years wine and brandy had virtually disappeared from the market and by the time the French industry recovered, Scotch whisky had taken the place of brandy as the preferred spirit of the masses.

Lastly, prohibition in the 1920s in the United States gave the Scots an incredible boost in blended whisky sales. Initially, prohibition resulted in a massive fall in whisky sales; however, the Scottish smuggling instincts kicked in and they jumped into the American market. The demand for illegal whisky sky rocketed and blended whiskies flooded the market.

An interesting bit of trivia – during prohibition Laphroaig was the only whisky that still could be sold legally by pharmacies because of its medicinal taste. It is said the only reason that this particular whisky survived prohibition was that the Government taxman couldn't imagine anyone drinking this stuff of their own free will.

By the end of prohibition the Scots had taken advantage of the lack of production in the United States and exported a bountiful supply of potent whisky. Before the First World War, all whisky was bottled straight from the cask. Then in 1916, as a wartime measure, it was ordained that the strength be reduced to 40% by adding water.

So when did all this start to change? Single malts began to gain popularity in the early 1990s with a large growth in sales in Japan, Hong Kong, Germany, Canada and particularly in the United States.

The problem by that time was that the demand for blends was so massive that most of the best malts were being used to produce them. The object of blending has always been to "soften" and make a consistent product in large quantities. Production could not keep up with the demand. More than 90% of the Scotch consumption in Scotland can be attributed to brands of blended whisky.

In the nineties, the baby boomer generation demanded more quality in their self indulgent lives. They wanted quality instead of quantity and so the sale of single malts was almost reborn. Rising disposable incomes have driven one of the major trends in the alcoholic beverage market. This means simply that if consumers cannot be persuaded to drink substantially more, they can be persuaded to drink more expensively. Those who are unfamiliar with whisky usually shy away from single malts because of their lack of product knowledge. Most do not realize that single malts are not a mass–produced product; rather, they are produced in small batches, by very skilled people and aged for years before the whisky is ready to be bottled and sold.

With this increased interest in single malts, smaller distilleries could now focus on the production and sale of their finest malts direct to the consumer. Was it the water, the terroir, or could it be the fine oak casks sitting in their quiet warehouses for years that lead to the single malts' popularity? These new breeds of independent purists are now the driving force in this segment of the industry, making a major contribution to the growth in popularity of single malts.

Over the last several decades, there has been a general trend within the Scotch whisky industry for consolidation of distilleries among the major players. These players began to purchase Scottish distilleries with the sole purpose of producing whisky for their top selling blends. A good example of this is Diageo's ownership of 27 distilleries, almost one third of the distilleries in Scotland, by August 2003. Many of these acquisitions were made solely for producing singe malts to be included in their top selling blends.

So, what I am saying is that many desirable single malts are not available to the consumer. The acquisitions and mergers in the Scotch whisky trade by the nineties were diabolical, leading many, myself included, to ask, "Is there really a monopoly commission?"

In my neck of the woods (Eastern Canada), and probably the rest of North America, I often hear, "Single malt enthusiasts moan that Lagavulin is out of stock yet again!" This is because Diageo uses 80% of Islay's Lagavulin production in their premium vatted pure malts. Many types of single malt such as Lagavulin are desirable for the blenders looking to create a premium marriage of whisky. Caol IIa, the largest Islay whisky producer, uses close to 100% of all their whisky for blends.

Many distilleries appear to be mothballed or out of action after the big boys took them over. In fact, many are still in production; however, you will never see the finished product. The final product is used in their blends and will never be available to the consumer. Millions of cases of Johnny Walker, Famous Grouse, Bells and Ballantines are sold every year. The consumers demand consistency in their favourite blended whisky and consistency of flavour is crucial to their success.

During the last decade, the Scots had enough of foreign companies buying up their national treasures. Entrepreneurs started to buy back or start new distilleries. This is when the Isle of Arran, Bruichladdich, Ardbeg and Bladnoch shook up the industry.

*Cardhu in your coke: "Are you loco amigo?"*

Another very silly trend occurred in this decade: young Spaniards demanding Cardhu in their coke. While I say silly, I do actually answer a question I am asked repeatedly at whisky dinners – why do young Spaniards put such a fine single malt in their coke? "Because they can!" is my reply.

Today, the savvy drinker will "brand their drinks" just as they brand their shoes or their cars. They will ask for Tanqueray and tonic rather than a gin and tonic. Driving their Beamers, dressed in the latest Armani fashion with a wallet full of euros – what is wrong with demanding the best malt in their coke? Whatever turns people on to malts is okay with me as long as they are continually experimenting with different malts. Furthermore, some whisky observers are analyzing their coke and their malts (as one would a fine wine).

In December 2003, Diageo provoked controversy over its decision to change its Cardhu brand Scotch whisky from a single malt to a pure (vatted) malt while retaining the original name and bottle style. Diageo took this action because it did not have sufficient reserves to meet demand in the Spanish market. (Cardhu is one of the main single malts used in their famous Johnnie Walker blends.)

All other firms in the Scotch whisky industry opposed this change. They claimed that changing the composition of the whisky (to a supposedly inferior product) while keeping the original name and bottle style would confuse drinkers and damage the reputation of single malt whisky and the Scotch whisky industry in general. Whereas the Scotch Whisky Association was unwilling to react, William Grant & Sons led other smaller distillers in the campaign to make Diageo reserve their decision. After a meeting of producers, Diageo agreed to make changes. As a result, the authority of the SWA was significantly undermined.

Just to make this matter more confusing, Diageo announced shortly after launching the Cardhu "Pure Malt," that they would be discontinuing this product and revert to a single malt.

Even so, at this time, Cardhu still seems very difficult in purchase in most counties. This entire hullabaloo resulted in the Scotch Whisky Association requesting that Westminster pass the following whisky labeling standards through Scottish Parliament as law so that no further controversy would result.

"Under the proposed new labels, it will be will compulsory for whisky producers to use the appropriate category name. The proposed categories are single malt Scotch whisky, single grain Scotch whisky, blended Scotch whisky, blended malt and blended grain Scotch whisky. Additional protection is proposed for traditional regional names, such as Highland, Lowland, Speyside, Campbeltown and Islay – a move designed to defend Scotch whisky from "unfair competition in its export markets".

## WHISKY'S IMAGE TODAY

In closing, a problem remains in that single malt whisky still suffers from a serious image problem among the younger set – whisky is associated with older drinkers. To younger drinkers, whisky appears to lack the mixability of other spirits such as vodka. As we all know the young do not willingly emulate what they perceive to be the drinking habits of their elders.

One of my main goals is to turn the younger set around so they will perceive that drinking single malts is sophisticated and trendy. Education with the help of media should be a starting point to expose them to a world of endless single malts. My experiences at several whisky events have shown that the interest among the younger set is there – it is just that they have no idea where to start.

So, the point of this book – keep it simple and to the point so that everyone, including the younger set, will have an idea of where to start and how to build their own palate to the point that they will be able to choose their own region and style.

*Karen Erasmus (Regional Sales Manager for Pernod Ricard, South Africa) is a dedicated whisky enthusiast. She is quoted on the website, Lafemme, as saying "the biggest market today in South Africa is whisky – and women are making up an increasingly large portion of that market. The image associated with whisky drinkers today is that of male or female professionals, trendsetters, and sophisticated social drinkers. Whisky is healthy because it's made with 100 per cent natural ingredients, is sugar free and is recommended for people suffering from high cholesterol, diabetes, and so on. Not many people realize it but the history and process of distilling whisky are more intricate than that of wine making."

(See Table "D" for the list Distilleries and Owners.)

**Chapter**

**2**

# Geography – Bonnie Scotland

*"Why did the inventors of the great game choose 18 holes to be a round of golf? Simple, there are 18 servings of whisky in a standard bottle." From the movie, Bobby Jones: "Stroke of Genius."*

Whether or not a Scottish caddie really said this doesn't matter – it makes sense to me. So before I get my clubs out for a practice swing for the upcoming season and ramble on about this amazing country, I should answer the most commonly asked question: what is a single malt whisky?

Whisky is much like beer. The masses drink the big names while the select few choose microbrews or, in Britain, cask conditioned ales on draft. The common denominator in the production of both whisky and beer is the use of barley. As Mike Myers would say in his best Scottish accent – if it's nae barley it's crap!

Some mega beer companies do not use any barley at all and the big whisky companies use only a proportion up to 50% in their regular blends. Many American beer companies still use barley; however, they add corn and rice to give their final mass produced product a clean and refreshing product with mild tastes. Barley has been and always will be the key ingredient for distilling beer and single malts. So much so, that in 1516, The Germans passed the "Purity Law" stating that their beer "must" be made with 100% barley and that law still stands today.

While traveling to London a few years ago, a fellow passenger asked me why I had chosen a German lager rather than a regular Bud or Coors. I explained that this beer was made with 100% barley and was much superior in taste. He looked very shocked and said he was a farmer and grew the very best corn for his cows, his prized possessions. If his corn was good enough for his cows, surely the corn was good enough for his beer! I nodded, while thinking that while corn may be alright for cows in this instance, I wasn't sure how great it was for us humans.

Ok – back to my point – what is a single malt? The definition of single malt is that it is the product from one single distillery and so has not been blended with whisky from any other distillery. The product must contain 100% malted barley (fermented with yeast) and distilled in traditional 'pot stills.' It may contain whisky from several production batches over a period of a couple of years.

Malt whisky has specific, sometimes very pronounced, flavours and aromas which come from the: (a) malted barley, (b) amount of peat used in drying it and again once aging is completed, and (3) the type of wood in which it matures. After a few years the whisky is sampled to see if it is good enough to be bottled as a single malt under the distillery's name. If not, it goes to a larger firm that combines it with other distillations, thus becoming a blend. The range of character of a single malt goes from deep, pungent, smoky and earthy to light, subtle, gentle and sweet. The use of 100% barley produces a far superior whisky to the common grain whisky found in blends.

The percentages of barley content vary with the production of blends. A typical blended whisky may contain between 15 and 40 different malt whiskies as well as grain whiskies. Although, in theory, there is no minimum proportion of malt whisky allowed in a blended whisky as long as there is some present, even the cheapest blended whiskies contain at least 5% of malt whiskies (although it is usually 10% – 40%).

Deluxe blended whiskies contain a higher proportion of malt whiskies – sometimes more than 50%. The majority of the malt whiskies added to the grain whisky provides the bulk and are usually of comparatively poorer quality than the "top dressings" used to fine tune the final product which give it depth and character.

That's enough technical stuff for awhile. The above topics will be covered in more detail later in the book. Back to Bonnie Scotland – the tiny country that produces so many diverse single malts for your enjoyment.

It's amazing how such a tiny country can produce a class of whiskies that are so very diverse and distinctive. Scotland is smaller than Croatia and just a wee bit bigger than the state of Maine. With only a small amount of working distilleries left in operation they can still produce a fantastic selection of whiskies.

Scotland seems to have a bit of just about everything and it's no wonder artists, songwriters and poets are caught up in the romance and beauty of this place. While the Scottish landscape is an inspiration for the creative sort, it's also a golf and fly fishing haven with a distillery lurking close by for those well needed refreshments. This country is one of the last unspoiled areas of the world. The contrasts of the rolling border hills, gentle coastal pastures, farmlands of Burns's Ayrshire, quaint fishing villages, to the Highlands – one of the dramatic landscapes in the world.

There are also many exceptional cities, such as historic Edinburgh, the industrial city of Aberdeen, the serenity of Inverness and the vibrant and modern Glasgow. All these cities are full of history, intrigue, myths and great whisky. A major example of how Scotland is changing is the city of Glasgow. Once known for being a bit of a "rough" place, Glasgow has been upgraded and modernized to such an extent that it is now listed as one of the top ten cities in Europe to live and work! Most points in Scotland are easy to get to and never too far away. One of my favourite places is Loch Lomond with its magnificent setting amidst grey mountains. It is only a 30 minute drive from Glasgow.

So you get the picture. Scotland is tiny – only 274 miles long and between 24 and 154 miles wide. Two thirds of the land is mountains with a rugged coastline to boot and I still have not mentioned the islands which number in the seven hundreds.

## THE TERROIR OF SCOTLAND

Who would have imagined a Scotsman using French words like "terroir" or each distillery and every cask having their own "DNA"?

If malt whisky were French it would, like wine, be legally divided into a dozen or so appellation contrôlées based on features such as analysis of water supply, specified barley types, and peat content.

The French have a word for the complex, almost mystical

interaction of bedrock, sub soil, soil and micro climate with the vine – "terroir." Often denounced by large producers as folklore, the differing influences on the vine, and therefore the wine character, has been well documented for over 1500 years to the extent that in Europe, and increasingly in the US and Australia, 'terroirs', or specific locations, are enshrined in law.

But does 'terroir' exist for whisky in Scotland? Would barley grown in different climates affect the taste or quality of the whisky? Do the air, the sea and the land shape that particular whisky?

## Absolutely!

No other spirit is as influenced by its "terroir" as the single malt. Scotch malt whisky is the taste imparted by the soils, the air, the water, the shape of the still, the wood in which it's aged, and so on. All single malts are distinctly different and this is what one has to remember when indulging in wee drams from the different regions.

## THE CLIMATE OF SCOTLAND

Scottish weather is variable, with four seasons often experienced in one morning as one moves through sunshine, showers, persistent rain, hail, gales and even snow. Despite variability in the weather, there are still common misconceptions held about the Scottish climate. It is not always raining and cold with three feet of snow. Depending upon season Scotland can be quite warm, even hot.

## RAIN AND SNOW

One of the most well known myths about Scottish weather concerns rainfall rate. It is often claimed the length and breadth of the country suffers from very high rainfall. In reality, the amount of rainfall not only depends upon season but also locale.

The differences in climate from the east coast to the west are remarkable. For example, a large piece of Scotland is made up of the rugged Highlands, where annual rainfall exceeds 1600mm (63 inches). In comparison, a huge proportion of Scotland has an annual rainfall of less than 800mm (31 inches). Moreover, many districts in the north and east of the country have a total rainfall of less that 250mm (10 inches) on average over the four summer months. A good example of this would be Speyside – known locally as "Little Mexico." Here there is only 20 inches of rain per year while the west coast and islands can have anywhere from 50 to 120 inches! This leads to another misconception – many people around the world believe London is always foggy and rainy. London gets about 25 inches per year – that's it.

One thing that does hold true is that Scotland experiences a greater number of days with snow than England and Wales. However, it must be stated that the majority of Scotland's population do not endure severe, snowy winters. Coastal areas and low lying parts of the Western Isles experience on average less than 10 days in the year with lying snow, while the north and northeast have between 15 and 20 days.

## DNA

These descriptions can now give you a sense of the diversity in such a small country. Imagine all that rain gushing through peat bogs from the mountains and saturating the vegetation. The climate ranges from the less damp and humid environment of Speyside to the islands which are strongly affected by not only the landscape but the strong, salty sea breezes.

All the above factors give each distillery its own individual DNA which means that no two single malts will ever be identical. Not unlike Grisham and the CSI team poking around on a crime scene to determine who did what! The terroir is the factor responsible for the varying tastes and nose of single malts. To demonstrate my point, note the differences between the following regions of Scotland:

(1) Island whiskies show a nose of salt (iodine) with traces of peat in most cases.

(2) The Lowlands have an abundance of good barley and spring water and this creates a softer, sweeter malt.

(3) In the Highlands you will note a touch of heather and smoke and these malts are much drier and less pronounced with a subtle profile.

These examples do not even include the "peaty monsters" of Islay.

## WHO'D 'VE THUNK IT!
## FRAUD IN THE WHISKY BUSINESS

When it was discovered that each brand of whisky has its own DNA, a major breakthrough in the battle against whisky counterfeiters was finally won. At Diageo, the problem is so great that they worked with trading standards officers to introduce a hand held testing kit for its products.

The new machine, which costs £5000 ($12,000 in Canada), solves the problem of how to identify faked whisky without laboratory analysis. A litmus test will identify a fake bottle of Smirnoff or Gordon's; however, strict rules governing Scotch meant that nothing could be added to the spirit to make the litmus test work. This new machine can complete a test in the outlet quickly and efficiently. It identifies the components in the whisky and quickly matches them up to those of the brand it claims to be.

## Chapter 3

# Scotland – The Designated Regions

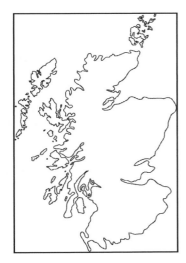

Once upon a time, not long ago the question regarding designated regions was quite simple. The Single Malt Whisky Society stated that there were to be only four designated regions; however, all this seems to be changing.

While many experts argued a case for Speyside being separated from the Highlands in the region's designation, a common thread was usually found to distinguish your favorite wee dram from another. Today it is a different story. The islands, for example, have become very popular with their own individuality: a trace of peat and salty seaweed is characteristic in their malts.

There are industry experts now asking for a maritime whisky category. Coastal malts will have a lot in common with island malts due to their proximity to the sea. However, Scotland is only approximately sixty miles across; consequently, all malts must have some sea air roaming about their distilleries when the wind is up. Another reason that throws off the four designated regions argument is that some Speyside distilleries are adding a touch of peated malt to their whiskies or going heavy on the first fill sherry casks.

All these factors have made it difficult to categorize regions and yet, it must be the main goal for the whisky industry to come up with an answer to this problem. One needs only to look at the wine business to see that we don't want to be bogged down like the French with their numerous appellations. However, the Australians are now finding after years of selling their wines on their country concept alone that consumers are increasingly eager to shop by region.

UK retailers have taken on this challenge and many have been innovative in merchandizing single malts by region including the Islands. Oddbins, one of the UK's multi award winning beverage retailers, even went the whole nine yards by including Orkney's Highland Park in the Islands section. Why not indeed! Orkney is one of the most independent of the Scottish islands and is steeped with fascinating history.

Some experts are debating that the regional designations should be scrapped altogether while others are demanding a style more like the wine industry with main regions and sub regions. In my line of work, this is the advice that I would give to a retailer. Merchandise your shelves by the following regions listed below from left to right.

## LOWLANDS

Geographical Area: The Lowlands lie in the southern part of Scotland ranging from the English border up to the Firth of Forth and from the Atlantic to the North Sea. There are four areas within the Lowlands: Central, East, West and the Borders.

Description: The soil is fertile and four large coalfields underlie the area. Here is Scotland's chief farming district and its largest cities. The hills are either rounded or have flat tops and are often capped with dark peat. The slopes are covered with grass as well as heather.

Whisky Profiles: The Lowland whiskies are usually gentle and moderately tangy due to the soft water and with a trace of peat. Whisky produced here is triple distilled and tends to be lighter in body and colour, mellower and, typically, have a dry finish. Their aromatic intensity is low, and tends to be grassy, green or herbal, with grainy and floral notes. Lowland malts are regarded by many as an excellent aperitif.

The Malts: Glenkinchie, Auchentoshan, Bladnoch, Littlemill, Glengoyne* and Deanston.*

Comments: These whiskies are light and easy drinking. If you want to attract a new consumer to single malts or a younger drinker, you can't go wrong with a Glenkinchie 10 or just about any other Lowland malt.

*Officially, Glengoyne and Deanston are considered Highland Single Malt Whiskies. These distilleries sit right on the border and these malts display all the characteristics of the Lowlands. However, the actual designation of who should take rightful ownership – the Highlands or the Lowlands is much in debate. Trade experts believe that these malts are Lowland malts and even the distilleries do not seem to mind being categorized this way.

## SPEYSIDE

Geographical Area: The Speyside derives its name from the River Spey. The region stretches from Aberdeen to Inverness and from the Eastern Highlands to the Moray Firth; over half of the distilleries in Scotland reside within the boundaries of Speyside, making it the unofficial capital of single malts. Its borders touch on the Northern, Western, and Eastern Highlands and one could easily argue that its products are the essence of Scottish whisky.

Description: Numerous rivers and streams flow through gentle foothills surrounded by pine forest wilderness. The water here is soft, clear, pure and sweet tasting. It is the foundation for most of Scotland's famous distilleries.

Whisky Profile: These whiskies of Speyside are quite sweet and high in estery tones. They are complex and sophisticated with great finesse and are generally favoured by blenders. In general, but not always, Speyside whiskies are made from very lightly peated malt. This will sometimes give them a light whiff of smoke. Speyside whiskies tend to be lighter than Highland and Islay whiskies; however, those matured in sherry wood can have a chocolaty richness.

The Malts: Tomintoul, Knockando, Cragganmore, Glenlivet, Glenfiddich, Benriach, The Balvenie, Glenrothes, The Macallan, Aberlour, Glen Grant, Longmorn, Glenfarclas, Dalwhinnie, Strathisla, Ardmore, Tamanvulin.

Comments: Speyside has two extremes while displaying common characteristics. Distilleries such as The Macallan, Glenfarclas, Aberlour and Glendonach are known for their sherried single malts while distilleries such as Glenlivet, Tamanvulin and Tomintoul are very gentle drams. The common factor here is a delicate sweetness and distinctive maltiness with little, if any, peat. Start with the lightest and work your way up to the big sherried malts.

If we really wanted to go overboard, Speyside could be split into a further ten sub regions as it is home to well over half the distilleries in Scotland. These subdivisions are: Bogie, Deveron, Dufftown, Fiddich, Findhorn, Inverness, Isla, Livet, Lossie, Rothes and Strathisla – unless you live in Speyside, who could remember all that!

*The Highlands are much like Speyside – a real bugger to sort out!*

eort

# THE HIGHLANDS

The area of Scotland known as the Highlands is the largest and most diverse category and includes a large area of the mainland and some islands (except Islay). This area is broken down into Eastern, Northern, and Western Highlands, the Midlands and Orkney.

## THE EASTERN HIGHLANDS

Geographical Area: The Eastern Highlands stretch from the North Sea to the Grampian Mountains in central Scotland to Monroseto Peterhead, a small coastal town at the mouth of the river Ugie.

Description: The weather ranges from overcast to rainy and, as is often the case in the British Isles, the horizon is where the grey meets the green.

Whisky Profiles: Earthy and full throated with exceptions, especially near the coasts. The whiskies are mainly light to medium weight and fragrant. They are smooth and sweetish, with a dry Highland finish and they are often malty and slightly smoky. These whiskies are sometimes fudge or toffee like with citrus notes and spice.

The Malts: Glengarioch, Royal Lochnagar and Fettercairn are fine examples of the East Highland style.

## THE MIDLANDS

Geographical Area: The Midlands region, technically a sub region of the Highlands, stretches along the Tay (Scotland's longest river) and includes the important towns of Perth and Dundee. This area is home to two of Scotland's largest blended whisky distillers, Dewars and Famous Grouse.

Whisky Profiles: The whiskies produced here are soft and delicate single malts.

The Malts: Edradour, Glenturret and Deanston.

# NORTHERN HIGHLANDS

Geographical Area: These Highlands stretch from the Moray Firth up to John O'Groats at the northernmost tip of the Scottish mainland.

Description: The Northern Highlands have the highest mountains in Britain and the deepest and longest inland waters. The region embraces both the most northerly and most westerly parts of mainland Britain and it has the lowest density of population. The Highlands are wild and picturesque. Their rocky, barren summits were chiseled by Ice Age glaciers and the rainfall of many centuries. Purple heather clothes the lower slopes in late summer. The valleys are usually steep sided glens, with a long, narrow loch at the bottom.

Whisky Profile: Highland Northern whiskies are usually light to medium bodied, quite complex and delicate. They tend to be dry, are usually salty and can be spicy.

The Malts: Tomatin, Clynelish, Glenmorangie, Dalmore, Balbair, Old Pulteney, Glenleigh and Glen Ord.

Comments: The North Highland distilleries are all on the coast except Tomatin which is in the southernmost part of the region. (Tomatin is included for convenience: its product has more of a Speyside character). The most northern is Pulteney which produces a delicious, fragrant, dry whisky, long referred to as 'the Manzanilla of the north." Then there is Clynelish – a sophisticated and complex whisky. It is a core malt in the super deluxe Johnnie Walker Gold blend.

# WESTERN HIGHLAND

Geographic Area: This region includes the land west of the Grampian Mountains in central Scotland, extends out to the Atlantic Ocean and falls down near Glasgow in the south. The Port of Oban ("Little Bay" in Gaelic) is also rightly referred to as the "Gateway to the Isles" and is the unofficial capital of the West Highlands.

Description: This is where the Highlands meet the Islands. These distilleries are nestled beneath the steep cliffs of the rugged coastline.

Whisky Profiles: Highland Westerns tend to have more peaty notes and often a firm, rounded character. These malts all have at least a whiff of smoke and a mildly phenolic flavour. If there is a uniting factor, it is the sweet start and the dryish, peppery finish of these whiskies. Ben Nevis is quite unusual and quite sweet with a remarkable aroma and flavour of coconuts.

The Malts: Oban and Ben Nevis

Comments: The region's style is malty and refined, light heather and lighter peat. The West Highlands are seldom used as a separate category from the Highlands.

Finally – Campbeltown, Islands & Islay are so much easier to sort out!

## CAMBELTOWN

Geographical Area: Located on the Mull of Kintyre, Campbeltown is situated at the extreme southeastern point of the mainland part of Scotland. The village of Campbeltown lends its name to one of the smallest appellations for single malts. At one point during the 1800s there were nearly 30 distilleries on this remote peninsula. Ships' captains, it was said, could find their way into Campbeltown port through the thickest fog, just by following their noses.

Description: This beautiful part of Scotland has a varied landscape. The peninsula has rolling farmlands, miles of beautiful, unspoiled beaches backed by spectacular dunes to wetlands and moors complete with wild heather and blueberries surrounded by deep primeval forests.

Whisky Profiles: These whiskies are quite briny/salty and tangy due to the exposed nature of the surrounding sea. The judicious use of peat insures a full pure maltiness and depth of flavour rarely matched by some of the better known regions.

The Malts: Springbank, Glen Scotia and Longrow

Comments: Campbeltown is such a diminished category now that it is shared by only two distilleries: Springbank and Glen Scotia, producing three whiskies. When there were more distilleries it was regarded as a halfway house between mainland and Islay styles.

## ISLAY

Geographical Area: Pronounced "eye-luh", this island is also known as "The Queen of the Hebrides;" Islay is the most southerly of the Hebridean islands off the west coast of Scotland. It is approximately 25 miles long north to south and approximately 20 miles wide east to west.

Description: Islay's natural resources include fertile soil, extensive peat bogs and wonderful soft peaty water all mixed with sea breezes. The situation of Islay, exposed to the full force of the Atlantic, has led it to become the site of a pioneering wave power station called Limpet. The climate on Islay is often more clement than the Scottish mainland owing to the Gulf Stream. At least a quarter of the island's surface is covered with peat.

Whisky Profiles: Its single malts are noted for their seaweedy, iodine like, phenolic character. It is a category in its own right due to the pungent, concentrated and peaty earthiness of the traditional style of whisky produced. Tasters speak of seashore and even medicinal dimensions to the richness of the prevailing character yet the whiskies have their own remarkable structure and balance.

The Malts: Ardbeg, Bowmore, Bruichladdich, Bunnahabhain, Caol lla, Lagavulin and Laphroaig.

Comments: Traditional Islay whisky is becoming very popular outside Scotland, although some distillers are choosing to lighten the style. The distilleries in the south of the island – Lagavulin, Ardbeg and Laphroaig – produce the most strongly flavoured, phenolic whiskies in Scotland.

The distilleries to the north – Bunnahabhain, Bowmore, Caol Ila and Bruichladdich – tend to be of a lighter character. Indeed some specify unpeated malt and draw their water directly from springs before it has had time to pick up much peat. In spite of this, the malts still taste peaty!

## THE WESTERN ISLANDS

This region consists of the Isles of Mull, Jura, Skye and Arran located along Scotland's rugged west coast. I have also included the Shetland Islands and Orkney in this category. Although there is no definitive "Western Island Style," there is the thread of peat and salt that runs through all of the malts produced here. See "Distillery Profiles" for detailed descriptions of each Island and their distilleries.

## ISLE OF MULL

The Isle of Mull is approximately 300 square miles in size and is the third largest island in the Hebrides. Mull's dramatic landscape has fluted, bare mountain flanks and volcanic cliffs contrasting with great sweeps of green glen and sheltered pastoral meadow. Here you will find Tobermory and their extremely peaty, Ledaig. The major part of the production is used in the blends of the group Scottish Leader and Black Prince, and about 50% is sold to other blenders.

## THE ISLE OF JURA

The Isle of Jura is the third largest of the Islands of Argyll with a population of less than 200. The island has a varied landscape but is dominated by the majestic peaks, moorlands rich in wildlife, trout–filled lochs, raised silver sand beaches with rocky shorelines and caves. Yet, for its size, Jura is the wildest, emptiest, and least tourist–oriented of Britain's inhabited islands. Nowadays the Islanders of Jura live on the east coast where the Jura Distillery is located.

## ISLE OF SKYE

Home of Talisker, it is the largest (1,735 sq km), and most northerly island of the Inner Hebrides. It has an irregular coastline, and many of its lochs are rimmed by lofty, sheer precipices. The climate is mild, and Skye is considered a resort despite its heavy rainfall.

## ISLE OF ARRAN

Arran is a small island, 20 miles long and 56 miles round, located off the southwest coast of Scotland. Palm trees grow here in the mild climate thanks to the Gulf Stream.

The name of this beautiful island means "peaked island" in Gaelic and it is often called "Scotland in miniature" for its range and wealth of scenery. A dynamic new force in the Scotch whisky industry, Isle of Arran Distillers is one of the few independent distilleries in Scotland.

# ORKNEY

Orkney is made up of 70 or so islands – exact agreement as to the total number is difficult as many are little more than skerries, that is, small, uninhabited islets. Of these islands only 16 are inhabited. Lying on latitude 59 degrees north – which is only 50 miles south of Greenland – Orkney is, at its widest, 30 miles from east to west and 53 miles north to south. Complete with green fields and hills, stone pinnacles rising out of the sea, rugged cliffs and sandy beaches, Orkney is an archipelago of 70 islands off the north coast of Scotland. Orkney has stone circles, burial mounds, and the best of the entire 5000– year old village at Skara Brae, preserved under a sand dune until 1850 when a violent storm exposed it. There are only 2 distilleries left – Highland Park and Scapa.

# THE SHETLAND ISLANDS

Shetland lies in the track of the Atlantic depressions and is bathed by the relatively warm waters of the Slope Current, flowing north along the edge of the Continental Shelf, so the climate is classed as temperate maritime. The effect of the Drift is to warm the climate in winter and cool it in summer so that temperatures vary only a little year round (5 – 15°C on average). It also rains two days out of every three. A great whisky needs a range of ingredients and conditions and all these factors have been proven that the Shetlands is the ideal place for the creation of a perfect dram.

## Chapter 4

# The Perfect Recipe – Barley & Water & Yeast

## BARLEY

Barley is a food cereal similar to wheat and oats. It has always been the primary raw material for conversion to malt. The preference for barley over other cereals is undoubtedly the fact that the corn or seed is covered with a straw like husk that is not removed by threshing and protects the grain during the process stages in malting. The husk subsequently serves as a filter in the mashing operations.

There is no legal obligation to use "Scottish" barley to produce Scotch whisky. Even if some producers would like to go back to the tradition, like Bruichladdich does, most of the distilleries are not concerned by the origin of their barley. Their main concern is that the sugar content be high and the price low. The combination of these two elements is often the only criteria in the choice of a variety of barley.

## BARLEY STRAINS

Each distiller has his own preference to the type of barley used. From 1970– 1985, Golden Promise dominated the distilling barley market. The Macallan has a unique flavor as it is the only distillery that continues to use 30% Golden Promise barley. Most distillers gave up on Golden Promise long ago because it is prone to disease and so they couldn't count on the supply.

In the last several decades experiments have been carried out to give the farmers varieties with higher yields and the distiller's higher amounts of fermentable sugars. Varieties such as Prisma and Chariot are now widely used; they have 7.5% more spirit per ton than Golden Promise. Although Scottish barley is considered the most suitable, due to the soil and climatic conditions, there is not enough to satisfy the industry demand.

If a distillery moves on to a new strain, it must be identical to its current one. Although the strain of barley is of little significance to the taste of the whisky, it does make up the all important DNA of the distillery and their final product.

Today only a handful of distilleries have their own maltings including Highland Park, Glenfiddich, Bowmore, Laphroaig and Springbank. Whisky specialists can provide distillers with more consistent malt made to their detailed specifications. These days barley is often purchased in bulk and shipped from overseas. A great deal of the barley used to produce Scotch whisky is being imported from England or South Africa.

## PEATED BARLEY

In the early '70s a decision was made to build a centralized malting plant alongside the distillery at Port Ellen to supply Islay. The new facility opened in 1973 and now supplies all the working distilleries on Islay and Jura. This facility uses drum malting with each of the seven drums holding 46 tons of barley. Germination takes five days, after which the green malt is dried in one of three kilns.

Today the majority of distilleries buy their malted barley from the large scale industrial maltings such as that at Port Ellen or Simpson's. These operate more quickly and efficiently than floor maltings, and the distiller can specify precisely the specifications of the malt received – all the way down to the exact degree to which it tastes of peat.

A combination of peat smoke and hot air is used to dry the grain and the exact amount of peating given depends on the distillery at which the malt will be used.

## TYPES OF BARLEY – TWO ROW & SIX ROW BARLEY

Barley grown for brewers and distillers is called malting barley, as opposed to feed barley, and is divided into two general types: 2 row and 6 row. The most obvious difference between a head of 2 row barley and a head of 6 row barley is the arrangement of the kernels on the barley head.

Two row is plumper and responsible for a softer, sweeter flavor. It is regarded as higher quality and long has been the standard in the traditional brewing nations. Six row barley is found more often in the United States and hotter Mediterranean lands. Europeans brewers are not alone in calling six row less refined; a beer made only with six row is more likely to taste grainy and will probably show chill haze because of excess proteins. In moderation, six row lends a firmness and husky character to beer, which some ale brewers prefer. (Chill haze is the cloudiness that occurs when unfiltered whisky is diluted with chilled water.)

Six row is less efficient (yielding less extract from a mash) but because of higher levels of diastic enzymes and protein it is better suited for mashing adjuncts, such as corn or rice, that lack those materials. Thus it was (and is) a perfect barley malt for the style (light lager, with adjuncts) beer that came to dominate the U.S. beer market in the 20th century.

Back to being a bit more technical (and I will be brief): A grain of barley consists of two main parts, the embryo and the endosperm.

- The embryo is the important part of the corn (barley) as all the organs which will develop into a future plant are present there in a modified form.

- The endosperm is the chief food storage organ of the seed from which the embryo draws its food supplies in the early stages of germination.

Also present in both the embryo and the endosperm are proteins and enzymes; present in both (to a limited extent) are substances known as proteins.

## WATER

Water is extremely important in whisky making and its effect depends on many factors. Does the water flow over peat bogs, or does it flow through granite? What are the influences of sea breezes from both the east and west coast? Does the water originate from springs or reservoirs? What is the mineral content: hard or soft?

Until a few years ago, water was considered the most important factor in the production of whisky. Today this "importance" factor is only about twenty percent with other components of whisky production having a lot more influence in the final taste.

Water is used in 5 processes:

1) in steeping during the malting process.
2) during mashing.
3) to cool the condensers or worm tubs.
4) to reduce the strength of the spirit prior to filling the cask.
5) to reduce the strength prior to bottling.

After illustrating the amount of rainfall in Scotland, we might not think to consider the problem presented to distilleries by drought. In 2003 Scotland experienced a rather severe drought.

Distilleries such as The Macallan and Talisker were stymied as to whether they should use another water supply. If they did, they had to wonder what would happen to their taste profile. Rather than take any chances, they reduced their production and continued to use the same water supply. The same situation has occurred in 2005 but to a lesser extent.

## YEAST

The yeast, crucial in triggering the chemical process by converting the sugars in the malted barley into alcohol, has little influence in flavour.

Yeast (brewer's yeast, often mixed with culture yeast) starts the fermentation process. The yeast constitutes a group of single celled fungi – a few species of which are commonly used to leaven bread and ferment alcoholic beverages.

The conditions need to be warm and wet, with a ready supply of the right food (sugars). Yeast cells can double in number in two hours – excreting carbon monoxide and, most importantly, alcohol. This phase lasts about thirty–six hours, during which the temperature rises to about 35°C. The temperature, combined with the level of alcohol which has been generated by now, causes the budding to slow down.

**Chapter**

**5**

# Smoke Gets in Your Malt!

The new growing army of peat enthusiasts is much like the hop heads of micro beer in the early nineties. Baby boomers that grew up with strong tastes like coke, burgers and curries are now hooked on the strong taste of hops. Talk about trends! First Australian Shiraz and now big peaty monsters! So what is all the fuss about? After all, peat is just decayed vegetation that's eight thousand years old in your wee dram. (You thought your favorite 15 Year Old in a cask was quite old!)

Peat bogs are found almost everywhere in Scotland as well as in Ireland, Canada and Germany. If you pick up a piece of peat, you are touching a bit of history that spans back to prehistoric times. You have much the same feeling if you were on Islay with its wide open spaces, lack of trees and hard sea breeze looking out for miles across the terrain of fens and peat bogs. There may be a lone figure digging with his special tool to a depth of 10 meters to slice the peat and stack it for drying. Care is taken to place the top layer back in its place to keep the environment in balance. This stuff is the first stage of transformation of plant matter into coal!

There are only a handful of these craftsmen left in Scotland and a worry is that the European Economic Community (EEC) and environmental bodies are looking for any excuse to ban this work of art. Let's hope not — where would we be without peat? Peat occurs uniformly across the Scottish landscape so it is no surprise that it has long been the traditional household fuel. If you were visiting Islay you would continually smell the peat mingled with the sea spray. Eureka! You may exclaim. Now I understand those nuances of iodine, salt and peat.

Peat bogs form where rain and snow directly feed an already high water table. As we know, there is no shortage of rain in Scotland. Peat can be found in many types of wetlands such as marshes, swamps, floodplains and coastal wetlands. These bogs become saturated with water, lack oxygen and nutrients and are high in acid. Peat is a dark fibrous material created when 'decomposition fails to keep pace with the production of organic matter'.

## THREE LAYERS OF PEAT

**Fogg** — The top layer, which is the lightest in colour and weight, contains the remnants of heather that is the distillery trademark.

**Yarphie** — The prized, deep brown middle layer that, with the fogg, is responsible for the maximum of smoke.

**Moss** — The very bottom, heavily compacted, near black layer whose flame is controlled by the fogg and yarphie.

Why would peat smoke make such a difference and have lines of people at whisky shows eagerly waiting to sample a peaty monster?

The trick is to make smoke, not flame! That wonderful peaty, smoky nose and taste on our favourite malt results from, in layman's terms, just the right amount of peat heated with coal, creating smoke and in turn, creating phenols.

Chemistry and the sciences were not my favourite subjects at school, so in terms that we will all understand, here is my "science" love story.

Phenols are compounds that are created when burning peat. These little beauties climb up within the smoke to the malting floor with hot steaming barley. Their sole purpose in life is to find the adorable barley husks. Once the phenols see the barley husks it's love at first sight and the husks have no option but to accept their new soul mate. Some of these phenols hang on through the distillation process and then disappear. However, others stay on through years of maturation and only disappear when you take that first sip from your wee dram.

Therefore, when seeing any peat level charts and numbers, one must take into account that the ppm's (phenols per million) quoted are at the malted barley stage. Through distillation and age, phenol levels will drop. The phenols in the malt are much higher than in the spirit or after aging and will reduce by over 60% in the final product.

The amount of peat and the area the peat is from is decided by each distillery and orders are sent to Port Ellen or Simpson's where the peated malt will be produced.

Talisker malts have peaty characteristics are all from the water flows through peat on the Isle of Skye. This would counter the comments being made today by experts that water is not important. The following chart shows the most peated malts including the number of phenols.

## PHENOL TABLE FOR PEATY MONSTERS

| Distillery | PPM |
|---|---|
| Bruichladdich | 5–8 |
| Bunnahabhain | 5–10 |
| Coal Ila | 30 |
| Bowmore | 20 |
| Laphroaig | 35–40 |
| Lagavulin | 40 |
| Ardbeg | 50 |
| Bruichladdich (Octmore) | 80 |

How many phenols per million (ppm) does not always determine the peatiest taste on the palate. Ardbeg has the highest ppms in their whisky and the new Bruichladdich 3D (not available in all countries) beats the lot. However, Ardbeg is far more subtle and has an array of many other flavors than Lagavulin where the peat really shows through.

On our distillery visits, we may marvel at the unique pagoda roofs and the chimneys of the original distilleries. Most of these chimneys are no longer used and the distilleries have turned the malting floor area of whisky production into pubs and restaurants as distilleries today are bringing in their peated barley from industrial maltings such as Port Ellen & Simpson's.

A colleague once mused that, sadly, industrial maltings by distilleries would lead to identical flavours in whiskies. In fact that is far from the truth. Master Distillers/Distillery Managers are perfectionists and take their art very seriously, much like a head chef decides on the exact amount of salt or herbs they use in their creations. Whisky producers work very closely with such manufacturers as Port Ellen in order to determine the perfect maltings for their distillery.

Cooley's Distillery in Ireland would have much preferred to use Irish peat for making their whiskies. By using Irish peat, they were not able to create the exact taste profile the distiller manager was hoping to achieve. They turned to the most popular areas of Scotland for peat and, finally (still not satisfied), finished with a peat they brought in from the northeast corner of Scotland. Only the distillery manager knows the why and the wherefore – and these magical secrets will be kept from mere mortals like me!

Today there are only a handful of distilleries that use peat fires to malt their own barley. At distilleries such as Highland Park, you can still witness huge strong Scottish men with arms like Arnie Schwarzenegger continually raking the malted barley. For most distilleries, this hand method of producing their own malt (grist) is simply not cost effective.

## Chapter 6

# Distillation

*Why do whiskies all taste different? The various factors include:*

**The Malt** – The malting method will change the aroma: smoky, if cooked over a peat fire, less notably so if a coal, wood or oil fired kiln is used.

**The Water** – In certain areas of Scotland the source is heavily charged with peat, which in turn transfers its taste to the finished product.

**The Still** – Depending on the size and shape of the still, the end product can vary enormously; a very tall still will generally produce a fine, elegant and subtle alcohol, while a smaller, short and fat still will produce a much more robust alcohol, richer in secondary tastes and aromas.

**The Cask** – A barrel which has been used for sherry and which still has the lees floating around will quickly turn a whisky ruby red and give it a strong, fruity, winey taste. A bourbon barrel will age much more slowly, preserving the clear colour of the whisky and allowing the tastes and aromas introduced by the still, water, malting, etc., to shine through.

**The Environment** – During maturation the barrel will 'breathe.' This will impart a specific flavour to the whisky, depending on the atmospheric conditions outside. A barrel which is stored in salty, sea air will produce a whisky with a hint of iodine.

The variations in local temperature also affect the aging process. A barrel subjected to large swings in ambient temperature will age much more quickly than one stored in a more stable environment.

**The Age** – There is such a thing as a whisky which is too old. Some expensive bottlings are not necessarily the best, and if the liquid spends too much time in the barrel it becomes woody. Too young can be strongly alcoholic and aggressive.

I really don't want to put you to sleep with myriad details and technical notes. All single malts are produced pretty much the same. The difference is all in their own terroir and casks which gives them their very own DNA identity. The stills play a big part but the actual process remains the same for all of them.

*How to Make a Single Malt Scotch (and not your Mother's recipe)*

1) First, you have to make your malt. Find a field of quality barley, cut it, thrash it and sift out the grain.

2) Leave this to soak in water until the grains begin to germinate.

3) Dry it in a malt kiln (oven). This is one of the first things that determine the flavour of the final product. Whether the grain is dried in a traditional peat fired kiln rather than a modern gas–

fired kiln will determine the peat induced, distinctive 'smoky' aroma found in many whiskies.

4) Grind the grain into grist – which looks very much like flour.

5) Move the grist to the mash tun and add to hot water at about 75°C and leave to 'mash' for a couple of hours. The mash tun gives the grist a jolly good stir and thrashing. The starch now changes to sugars and produces a sweet, gooey liquid known as the wort.

6) Cool the resulting sugary liquid, add yeast, and leave for 4 or 5 days to ferment, producing an alcohol similar to beer at approx 7 or 8% Abv. The process so far has taken about two weeks and we are still at a similar product to beer.

*Now for the exciting bit – this liquid is now transferred to the stills and at this point we are ready for the process that makes whisky unlike any other product.*

7) Take this liquid, pour it into a large copper kettle (still) and heat it up to around 85 – 90°C. The alcohol will evaporate before the water, so collect all evaporated liquid by condensation. The output will be a liquid at about 25% Abv.

8) Take this liquid and run it through a second still, raising the Abv to 65 – 70%.

9) Throw this spirit into a barrel and wait.

10) When you feel that it is old enough, and after thorough testing, add water to the whisky to lower the Abv to around 40%, and pour into bottles.

11) Pour yourself a glass, light the fire and sit down in your favorite chair (with the dog of course) and savour this liquid gold!

Easy so far! Now for the real mystery (step #7). The pot stills that are used in whisky production are much like brewing a cuppa tea! Stills are big kettles. Think of boiling the kettle in your kitchen. Once the water reaches boiling point steam appears. Now, if you could cool down the steam it would change in to vapour droplets.

The immediate steam would not be up to snuff for your cup of tea as most of us like to wait until the water has boiled sufficiently but we don't want to wait forever. If we boiled the kettle almost dry we would have a burnt sort of taste in our tea. The perfect boil is what makes a great cuppa tea. I bet the distilleries wish it was that easy!

The pot still is filled to a certain capacity with wash so it can be boiled off. The alcoholic vapours rise to the top of the swan neck, pass over and run through cold pipes which condense them back to liquid. Perhaps the greatest advantage of using a pot still for distilling is that of its inefficiencies, it preserves much of the flavors and body derived from the mash.

In the case of the Pot Still, the design of the still, the height of the head (or top) and the angle of the wide diameter pipe, or lyne arm, connecting the head to the condensing unit, are all very important and have an effect on the final product. Each still has a large hatch on the top of the base of the still, the 'man door,' for inspection and cleaning. Further up the neck can be seen a small glass porthole which allows inspection of the contents of the still to ensure it does not rise too far up the neck and boil over.

The stillman is one of the most important aspects of making good malts and is one of the few areas left in whisky production that remains a mystery. The copper stills are even more mysterious. They may be fat and dumpy or long and thin with many variations in between. If the distillery ever had to replace a pot still, the new still would have to be a carbon copy of the old one – including dents and cobwebs. There is a fair variation in the design of pot stills and distilleries will vigorously defend the design of each as contributing something unique to the final product. This belief is now being disputed as having nothing to do with the character of the final product.

That is the basic concept of distillation, though the process is far more intricate than that. The stillman is a vital component in making great whisky. A keen eye and nose with years of experience are required.

### *"The second cut is the deepest."*

Stills are usually heated internally by a steam heater, which is a coil of tubing conveying steam. Occasionally, direct heating of the still over a peat or coal fire is found, using a rummager. The rummager is a series of chains connected to a revolving arm inside the still and then connected to the wash still. This prevents any particles of unfermented matter or yeast from settling and sticking to the still and being scorched by the fire underneath. There are still a few distilleries using coal or gas fires for their stills such as Glenfiddich and Glenfarclas. Glenfarclas tried using the steam process and found that this method changed their taste profile and reverted to using fuel.

Within every distillation, the distillate is divided into three cuts of which only the second cut, the heart of the run, will be used. The first, also called heads (foreshots) and the last fraction, known as tails (feints), are sub standard and will be redistilled together with the next batch of low wines.

We do know that the first spirit, known as the "head," is not good enough, and is sent back to try again. The "middle" is what the stillman is looking for which contain little impurities. The average amount of this middle taken is about 24%. There are exceptions, such as at the Macallan Distillery where the stillman only takes about

16%. The "tail" follows and that is sent back for a further try.

The stillman will capture the spirit in a cabinet with a viewing window and a small door where he can take samples for nosing and appearance. The middle part (heart) is what the stillman is waiting for and he will work his magic and take the required percentage. The middle cut is a clear liquid of up to 70% Abv.

Whisky experts, when describing this process at dinners and seminars, will give a brief overview of these three cuts. To keep it simple, they will say the first and the last cut are the baddies and the middle cut is what they need. However, the character of each whisky comes from the time the stillman takes to run the foreshots and the feints. Then how long do they take to run the middle cut? If you kept distilling, the result would be pure alcohol, like vodka, which is not what they want.

The special characteristics come from esters, acids, and phenols known as congeners which are the whole point. Hence the reason why the middle cut (heart of the run) is not really discussed in detail at seminars. Even the experts have no answer to this; it's all up to the stillman!

May I have some please? Well actually the spirit at 60 plus percent is surprisingly delicious while being a tad strong. However, the answer is no. You must wait for probably ten years or more and let the wood and the warehouse environment perform their magic.

## Chapter 7

# The Irish were first!

In this chapter, I will be discussing the other styles of whiskey. You will notice that I am now using "e" in the word whiskey.

There are two Gaelic translations of the words Uisge beatha (water of life). When translated in Irish Gaelic, the word whiskey contains the "e." When the Scots translate the word – there is no "e". In keeping with tradition, most countries outside of Scotland tend to use the Irish version; however there are exceptions such as Glen Breton Whisky of Canada and Whisky Breton of France.

## IRISH WHISKEY

Now I am not sure the Irish would appreciate being included with all the other whiskies. After all, they say they invented the stuff! The story goes that Irish Monks passed through Islay on their way to mainland Scotland to spread Christianity and brought this magic liquid with them.

The Irish have always been known for producing excellent blends in a lighter style. Most distillers in Ireland triple distill their whiskey giving it a lighter, smooth taste than the whiskies of Scotland. Most Irish whiskies are blends (produced in Ireland, of course) and peat is almost never used in the malting process. This results in a whiskey with a smoother, sweeter flavour. In most Irish whiskey, the smoky, earthy overtones of Scotch are absent.

Irish whiskey comes in several forms. Like Scotch, there is single malt whiskey (100% malted barley distilled in a pot still) and grain whiskey (grains distilled in a column still). Grain whiskey is much lighter and more neutral in flavor than single malt and is almost never bottled as a single grain. It is instead used to blend with single malt to produce a lighter blended whiskey.

Today, thanks mainly to Cooley's distillery in County Louth, there is a revival of Irish single malts with the likes of the Tyrconnell and their unique peated Connemara. The principal difference is that the mash is made using some unmalted barley, and the spirit is distilled three times (triple distilled). Unique to Irish whiskey, to which there is no Scotch counterpart, is pure pot still whiskey (100% barley, both malted and unmalted, distilled in a pot still).

It is this third distillation that gives "Irish" its different taste. At the Midleton Distillery in County Cork, depending on the desired outcome the spirit may have been distilled as many as 5 times. The distilled spirit at this stage still has a long journey ahead of it before it can be truly called whiskey.

Given that peat is not generally used in the malting process, it lacks the smoky edge of Scotch.

## BOURBON

The Americans love their scotch but love their bourbon even more. Bourbon is a corn whisky with a minimum of 51% corn and must be produced in the United States. Bourbon must be distilled at less than 80% Abv. (160 proof) and is then aged for a minimum of two years in new charred casks. Generally, most bourbon bottles at four years.

Almost all bourbons come from Kentucky but it is not a legal requirement. The name "Bourbon" comes from a county in eastern Kentucky, which in turn was named for the Bourbon kings of France who had aided the American rebels in the Revolutionary War. Ironically, now, it is a "dry" county.

You will also see on the labels the words "sour mash." Developed by Dr. James Crow, this process calls for each new fermentation to be conditioned with some amount of spent beer. This spent beer is fermented mash that has been separated from its alcohol in much the same way that sourdough bread is made from starter. The acid introduced by using the sour mash controls the growth of bacteria that could taint the whiskey. As of 2004, all straight bourbons use a sour mash process.

## TENNESSEE WHISKEY

Tennessee whiskey is a type of American whiskey produced in the state of Tennessee. It is generally similar to bourbon in that it is composed of a mash of 51 – 80 % corn or maize and aged in new, charred oak barrels for a minimum of two years.

The difference between the two is that Tennessee whiskey must undergo the "Lincoln County Process." This process requires that the whiskey be filtered through an approximately 10 foot thick layer of maple charcoal. This step is considered to give the whiskey a distinctive flavor and makes it unusually mild. The process itself is named for Lincoln County, Tennessee, which is where the Jack Daniel's distillery was originally located.

Are you getting the common thread? It's all about the grain used and unless there is 100% barley it's not a single malt. Now you have it – rye must be made from rye. Well, not really. Canadians still ask for rye and yet the whiskey will be made from corn or wheat. There are still some true rye whiskies made in the USA with at least 51% rye grain. Canadian whiskey asked for by the name of "rye" is a blend and mostly from corn.

## BLENDED SCOTCH

As previously mentioned, blended whisky (Scotch) makes up 90% of whisky sales today. The reason blends are so popular are: (1) consumers do not want to spend the money and (2) the consumer has no product knowledge and thus take the easy way out and purchase "big" name blends.

A whisky drinker who appreciates good single malts will buy blends during the week at their local pub and hoard the single malt for the weekend. Friends pop around on the weekend and the wine starts flowing and of course you really don't want to share your single malt with friends. It costs a packet and unless they really appreciate it, there is no way you are going to open that bottle of 20 year old single malt. Alas, this is no way to increase single malt sales and one can only hope that distilleries can offer lower priced drams in the future.

Don't get me wrong. Blending is a fine art and very big business. When the Coffey (continuous still) was invented in 1831, a dramatic change came about in the scotch industry. Every day you can produce mega amounts of whisky that will be high in alcohol, smooth, and without many of the tastes found in single malt with the Coffey.

A blended scotch whisky may contain a combination of whiskies from over 40 or 50 different barley and grain distilleries. The normal ratio of malt to grain is 60% grain to 40% barley. The percentage of malt used will determine the quality and smoothness of taste and character. Blenders do their job strictly by smell (no tasting). Master Blenders combine the various malts and grain whiskies to produce a consistent "brand style."

Vatted malts, or pure malts, are a different kettle of fish entirely and this term may change again by the time this book goes to print. A vatted malt is a marriage of single malts from different distilleries and never uses the "blend" word. Vatted malts contain only malt whiskys – no grain whiskys. They are usually distinguished from other types of whisky by an absence of the word 'single' before 'malt' on the bottle, and by the absence of a distillery name. The age of the youngest whisky in the bottle is the one used on the label – so a vatted malt marked "8 Years Old" may easily include whiskies over 30– years old.

It may appear to the reader that I flew through this lot, and you would be right since this book is focused on single malts. There are many fine blends, vatted malts, bourbons, ryes and the like. A person's preference is all about lifestyle. That is, it is up to you to choose whether you'd like to take the time to savour a fine single malt or if you'd rather go for scotch on the rocks. Either way, it's your choice.

# WHISKY (E) GOES GLOBAL

There are more and more countries entering the world of single malts. Australia, Japan, France, Wales, and even England are just a few of the newcomers. Most of these distilleries are still a bit young and, if their whiskies are released early, would have to include caramel to take out the fire. Early signs predict these newcomers will have some cracking single malts in a few years.

One unusual location for a distillery is Nova Scotia, Canada and the Glenora Distillery. They have just celebrated their 10th anniversary and may be considered old in this list of pioneering single malt countries. They have done everything according to Scottish standards and practices including using Scottish production equipment, imported Scottish barley and bourbon casks. There is a little something different about Glen Breton Rare, which is hardly noticeable unless you're a canny expert from Scotland. There is a faint nose and taste of maple as maple trees line the brook which feeds the distillery spring water. The following is a partial list of other countries and their single malts:

- ☐ Australia & Tasmania: Sullivan's Cove Premium (40%)
- ☐ Canada Glen Breton Rare: Glenora Distillery (43%)
- ☐ France: Whiskey de Bretagne NAS (41%)
- ☐ Germany: Piraten Whiskey (40%)
- ☐ Holland: Distilled Old Maltky (35%)
- ☐ India: MacDowell NAS Single Malt (42.8%)
- ☐ Japan: Suntory 12yo 'Yamazaki' (43%)
- ☐ New Zealand : Lammerlaw 12yo Cask Strength (50.5%)
- ☐ Poland: Old Family Whiskey NAS (40%)
- ☐ Switzerland : Swissky NAS Single Malt (42%, OB)
- ☐ Turkey: Ankara NAS Malt Viski (43%)

# Casks – The Perfect Marriage

The white oak tree that is used exclusively in production of bourbon casks is found in Missouri, Tennessee and Kentucky. Oh, the sounds of bluegrass music, the taste of a little moonshine, and the spectacular landscape of the Ozark Mountains with miles and miles of untouched forests. The only tree that we are interested in is the white oak. This treasured tree is cut at about 70 years old and taken to the cooperages for cutting and seasoning.

The cut staves are left outside to season in the sun and rain to remove the tannins and oak lactones. Once this seasoning is completed, the staves are placed in a steam box for 15 minutes to prepare the wood for bending.

Now that the oak is seasoned and steamed it goes to the cooperage to be made into barrels. The oak staves from which barrels are made were originally softened over a small fire in order to bend them into the requisite curved shape. These days, the wood is softened with steam. But tradition is not ignored, for it turns out that the toasting associated with the old way of bending staves also contributed to the flavour of its contents. To reproduce the effect the insides of the barrels and the inner surfaces of the barrel heads are toasted.

Bourbon casks are charred (burnt) on the inside which creates a thin charcoal layer that the spirit filters through during maturation. The magic for the bourbon producer is called the red layer – the thin zone under the blackened char where the sugars in the oak are caramelized and where vanilla like compounds are created. Charring caramelizes those sugars, giving us the final product.

In Scotland bourbon casks are known as hogsheads and hold approximately 250 liters of liquid. Since these hogsheads are smaller than sherry casks, the spirit makes a good amount of contact to the wood.

Once the whiskies have matured for three to five years, depending on the producer, they are shipped to Scotland where the distilleries have a first refill which is discussed in further depth in a minute.

Sherry casks became very scarce after the Spanish Civil War and the industry began to move over to bourbon casks. As well, in 1964, the US Congress passed a law that all bourbon would have to be produced in new, white oak casks. This new law opened up the doors to the Scotch whisky market and the whisky distilleries began to purchase the US casks.

The result of savouring a fine scotch from a bourbon cask are the tastes of vanilla, nuts and smoke. Generally speaking, the whisky is not overwhelmed by any lingering influences of bourbon. It is a perfect match, allowing the whisky to stand out, while enjoying the delicate tastes and aromas.

Sherry casks are a different story. Galicia in Northern Spain has an abundance of white oak trees. Once they reach 100 years old, the trees are cut and shipped to the town of Jerez in Southern Spain where the casks will be produced.

At one time, sherry casks were easy to come by because of the popularity of sherry in the UK. These casks were shipped in bulk to England where the sherry was aged and bottled. The empty casks were then sold to the distilleries. The civil war in Spain created a shortage of sherry casks just after prohibition had ended in the USA. To overcome this problem, the Scottish distilleries turned to the United States and bourbon casks became the solution.

Unlike bourbon where only one style is produced, sherry is not quite so simple. There can be many styles of sherry all at different ages such as oloroso, fino and palo. Furthermore, the cask may be used repeatedly.

So back to Jerez! Wood is seasoned much like the bourbon producers, however, after steaming the staves into shape, a "toasting process" rather than "charring" is applied which will wake up the wood. A larger cask is used with a capacity of 500 liters and is known as a "Sherry Butt." Sherry is more dominant than bourbon in its marriage with whisky. From a whisky of a first refill sherry cask you will expect to find flavours such as nutty, spicy and toffee. The whisky will offer more depth and sweetness. It all depends on which sherry and for how long and how many times the cask has been used.

## WOOD POLICY TODAY

The most important factor in the development of the single malt category is casks. For over one hundred years, whisky producers have known good oak casks are the ticket to good whisky. The difference between producers is in their approach to finding premium casks and how they unite one cask with another. Today many distilleries have a wood policy. This means that they have a foolproof system to ensure the distillery knows exactly what they are purchasing.

A distillery has many questions when purchasing casks. For example, they must know how many times the casks have been used and for which product. Also important is the quality and type of wood. In asking these questions, the producers are trying to determine which cask will influence the matured single malt to further enhance the flavor profile.

To illustrate how far the industry has developed in recent years, I will use The Macallan as an example. Sherry casks are used at Macallan. It is a reputation they enjoy and with many of their whiskies being from first refill sherry casks, their malts have a distinctive taste. To ensure quality and consistency, they went all the way back to the oak tree and bought their own forests! Well, not quite; however, they do buy direct from the timber company.

The wood is then shipped to the Spanish bodegas and left to season for several months. Casks are made and filled with sherry, mostly oloroso style. After maturing in Spain, the casks are then shipped to Scotland and are ready immediately for their new partner – whisky. During shipping, the sherry casks are still filled with sherry and are kept upright.

Once they reach their destination, the sherry is discarded – presently we do not have a reliable source as to what actually happens to the sherry. The empty casks which now have a significant sherry character are filled with whisky. Of course, not all distilleries have such resources. However, they have still found ways to be thorough in their search for quality casks.

While it seems logical to assume that a first refill cask is better, it depends entirely on the single malt produced and the distillery manager's goal in taste profile. Remember, sherry is quite a dominant partner and many of us prefer a whisky with little influence from anything outside the norm. To reach the correct partnership for particular malt, a second, third or fourth refill cask may be used.

All the focus on ensuring quality of casks in the area of development is the finishing. A single malt, after a certain age, may be determined by the distillery manager to either lack a certain "je ne sais quoi," or to be not quite right for their customers.

**THERE ARE 3 TYPES OF CASKS USED:**

**Fresh Sherry Casks:** Uses the solera system of production, which consists of a series of wooden casks (called butts) containing sherry, usually placed in rows according to age. Traditionally, the most mature wines are in butts on the bottom row. With this system, there are very few spare casks available and now the supply of fresh sherry casks has been dramatically reduced. The Spanish are now using American oak to age their Sherries.

**Bourbon Casks:** Since prohibition, bourbon production law ensures that oak casks can be used only once for maturation of bourbon – these redundant casks (200 litres) are dismantled in Kentucky and shipped to Scotland where they are reassembled now as a 250 litre. Today, 90% or more of the casks used for filling with whisky are ex–bourbon hogsheads. The more subtle flavours from bourbon casks can best show off the true attributes of a well made whisky.

**Refill Casks:** All casks are re coopered to keep them in use for as long as possible. These casks are used for three or four fillings (or more) which creates a reduced influence on the contents. The colour and flavour imparted is reduced each time the cask is used. A third or fourth refill of bourbon will have less extractives to contribute. This has absolutely nothing to so with saving money, it is rather the distillery's desire with certain single malts to require less of a dominate partner in the marriage of a particular single malt

Having spent many years in sherry or bourbon casks and a final year in cognac, port, or calvados casks, the profile of the whisky will certainly change. Recently distilleries have broadened their search to include wineries where burgundy (clarets) casks have been tried and today Bordeaux, Italian Tuscans, champagne and who knows what else are in the mix. They even recently tried ale from the UK to mixed reactions, mostly poor.

The new trends in single malts are cask finishing along with peaty monsters. As with peat I hope the cask finishing will improve and offer a wider variety to the customer rather than the focus being on marketing.

A perfect example of this new finishing trend is Springbank Longrow 10 Year Old. This single malt has spent 8 years in sherry/bourbon casks and two years in a Royal Tokaij cask (Tokaij is a desert wine from Hungary). How on earth would you know this was a single malt to consider for your whisky cabinet (a pleasant journey no doubt)?

The message here is simply to continue making the single malt category exciting. It does not mean the whisky is superior finished in an unusual cask or that a port finish will dominate the flavours – it will not. Variety, however, is the spice of life.

I am sure by now I have totally confused you. To make all this even more baffling I will say that there has been a relatively new development in the rebuilding of the cask. The cooperage will actually rebuild both bourbon and sherry casks and use a selection of staves from both. Who can tell from research or even visits to the distillery the percentage of staves used in casks when the staves are made from both?

At the end of the day, I move that we allow the Scottish distilleries to keep some of their timeless secrets and they will continue to surprise us with their golden nectar.

# Warehousing – Home Sweet Home

The type of storage is also an important factor in the life of a cask of whisky. We must consider the type of warehouse, the location of the warehouse and even the location of the cask within the warehouse. Whether or not the warehouse is close to the sea or inland will affect the outcome of the whisky. We must even take into consideration the conditions inside the warehouse such as humidity levels. Estimates vary, but it is believed that around three quarters of the taste of malt whisky comes not from the malted barley, water or peat used in its initial production, but rather from the cask in which it is matured.

Once the spirit has been put into casks it is moved off to the bonded warehouse. Here the spirit spends the legal minimum of three years before it becomes scotch quietly interacting with, and reacting to, the wood of the cask. Perhaps twelve or more years will pass before it can become a notable single malt whisky.

**Three types of storage systems are used in Scotland:**

1) Dunnage (traditional)

2) Racking

3) Commercial (pallets)

Dunnage is the most traditional method of storage and widely seen as the ultimate accommodation. These are low rise warehouses with thick brick or stone walls with a slate roof. They provide excellent air circulation to keep temperatures more stable. Casks are usually stacked to a maximum of three high and all casks are carefully numbered and inventoried.

Racked warehouses are a concept from the 50s. These buildings were built on a large scale and usually constructed with brick or cement blocks with a tin roof. The casks are racked from 8 to 12 barrels high on steel rails. Temperature changes from summer to winter are more common in a racked environment. Furthermore, racked warehouses have large bay doors and usually kept open for forklifts which promote more temperature fluctuations. Experts believe that temperature changes and variations will affect the character of the whisky while not affecting the quality.

Every cask breathes while it matures. Since wood is naturally porous, some of the whisky evaporates out of the barrel during aging – this is known as the "Angel's Share." Approximately 2% of the cask's content per year is lost to the angels! As the temperature rises, evaporation is likely to follow suit and can typically reach 2.25 % Abv of a cask's total contents per year.

The alcohol and water simultaneously decline in both alcoholic strength and volume. Meanwhile, the evaporation rate slows down as alcoholic strength declines. This means a whisky barreled at 63.5% Abv may reach 58% Abv after 12 years, 56% after 18 and so on.

Humidity levels are yet another factor in the outcome of the final malt. With higher humidity levels, condensation will seep through the cask. Experts are not sure what this does to the malt although many believe a slower rate of maturation is achieved.

Location of the warehouse also plays a major part in the aging of the whisky. There are areas of Scotland that have specific microclimates that affect the aging process. If the warehouse is located close to the sea, there will be a higher rate of humidity that would promote higher levels of oxidation. Higher levels of oxidation yield more pronounced mint, vanilla and floral notes along with fruitiness such as pear drop, lemon, baked apple and apricot.

Despite all this, the extent that warehousing has on the overall quality of the whisky is still somewhat of a mystery.

## Chapter 10

# Bottling – Ready to Buy!

### MARKETING, MARKETING, MARKETING!

Look at how French wine sales have plummeted to a historical low in the last decade – did they all of a sudden start producing bad wine? I think not.

If you are going to purchase a wine to be shared with friends you should learn everything you can about this particular wine. At one time, the older generation, to which I belong, would buy "a sexy little Cote du Rhone from the 1978 vintage." According to my wine guide this is quite a good vintage. Consulting wine guides does not seem to be in vogue any longer.

The French had already claimed rights to regional wine terminology. When the Australians started to make a name for themselves in the wine business, the only names they were left with were the names of the grapes – Merlot, Syrah etc. What a brilliant concept! The consumers could actually see on the label what kinds of grapes were used to make the wine. Most French wine labels only list the region and not the grape. Today's consumers want a "Merlot" and if they can't find a label that says that (like the French) then they will find one that will (like the Australian's). Lately, however, the French have woken up and started imitating the Australians.

When it comes to labeling, scotch is still out there in the twilight zone. Labels are difficult to read and tell you very little. Vatted malts/pure malts and blends are even worse. Why can't they tell us in which casks they have matured? Most single malt labels just don't cut the biscuit, with little or no information on the distillery, its location or taste profile. It has taken me several years to research and develop my "Savvy Shopper's Guide" located in the back of this book to help sort out some of the mysteries. Like Australian wine–makers, there are some whisky producers with excellent labeling. The traditionalists are starting to realize without explicit information to the consumer on their labels they are losing customer confidence – and cash!

For example, when looking at the label of the Balvenie Double Wood 12 year old we see that the first cask is a "**traditional**" whisky oak. We would assume "traditional" is referring to a first fill bourbon cask! The second cask states that it is an original sherry cask. The latter is more in line to what the consumer would like to see.

I recently read a description with regards to The Macallan Fine Oak Range of single malts. "The Fine Oak family is a lighter whisky which is matured in European and American oak casks which have previously held sherry or bourbon," according to the distillery. From my research, the fine oak range is predominantly bourbon casks or new American oak casks. It is a fine whisky – why not give the consumer more correct information!

## BOTTLING

There are only four distilleries that have their own bottling plant at the source. To the purists, this is very important as this means water used to reduce cask strength is the same water used in the other four processes. The four distilleries that bottle at the source are: Bruichladdich, Springbank, Glenfiddich and Loch Lomond. They bottle at the source because they firmly believe that their water maintains their taste profiles. Bottling plants on the mainland are now forced into using demineralised water through European regulations. You therefore do not have any minerals or any imperfections in the water. It's pure, but not from source. Knowing the water source is extremely important for DNA fingerprinting and authenticity will make a difference.

## CHILLFILTERED VS NON–CHILLFILTERED

Non–Chillfiltered is the latest rage in whisky. In fact all whiskies were made this way before World War l.

Imagine the demand for good liquor in the USA after prohibition. The quality of the domestic whisky (bourbon) was really quite poor. Those with money and, in particular, the Hollywood stars were aware of a good scotch and quite happy to pay the price for imported whisky.

Yet, because of the American tendency to pop liquor in the fridge, regardless of the climate, the whisky would develop floaty lumps. None too appetizing! And so chillfiltered whisky was born.

## CHILLFILTERED

Distilleries had to come up with a process to prevent hazing, and since the USA was and still is their best export market, chillfiltration was born. This also helps to keep the single malt consistent. A drawback is that the removal of impurities also means the removal of some of the taste.

Chillfiltration is an industrial process designed to remove "esters" in whisky, which could form hazes and deposits when stored at low temperature. The whisky is chilled to near 0°C (32°F) and then passed through a fine filter. This removes some of the compounds produced during distillation or extracted from the wood of the cask, and prevents the whisky from becoming hazy when chilled, or when water or ice is added.

However, chillfiltration also removes some of the flavour and body from the whisky; some consider chillfiltered whiskies inferior for that reason. By chilling the whisky, various proteins coagulate and are removed by plaque filtration – rather than potentially forming an undesirable haze or clouding in the bottle.

## NON– CHILLFILTERING (NCF)

With the esters and important proteins left in the whisky, you will experience a more full bodied and flavourful malt. Just keep in mind: you will have a hazy dram if it is refrigerated.

## AGE STATEMENT

The age stated on a bottle is the amount of time that the youngest whisky in that particular batch was stored in wood. On all single malts, the age on the label represents the youngest whisky that is in the bottle. Some distilleries are introducing younger bottlings (often with no age statement) for consumers who wish to sample their product at a more competitive price.

Competitively priced single malt with no age statement may contain whiskies of less than ten years. Such a vatting is still a single malt, because all the whisky comes from one distillery.

Older whisky is not necessarily superior; it will take on its special taste profile through the amount of time aged in one or more casks. For example, the distiller may have finished the single malt in a different cask such as port. The alcohol content also drops while in the cask, so older cask strength whiskies are generally bottled at lower proof than younger ones. Malt whisky does not change once bottled, except to deteriorate if not stored correctly (that is if it is exposed to temperature shifts or sunlight) or if the cork deteriorates and allows leakage/evaporation.

Sometimes it's tough for all of us to move away from tradition as information is handed down from our grandparents and parents. It was not long ago we believed only the French and Italians made the best wine. However, time never stands still and the same can be said in the whisky business.

I find that in my end of the trade the most frequent comment that I hear is, "there is no age statement on this whisky, why would I buy it?" I also hear, "if it's not at least 10years old it must be too young or it's too expensive for its age."

In Scotland, some distilleries are so confident of their young guns that they are actually making an age statement of eight years. Why wait for that so called "magic 10" when your whisky is so good at eight? Macallan lead the way with an eight year old; Littlemill 8 is currently much sought after. I can certainly attest to the quality and smoothness of the Macallan 8. Curiously, this eight Year Old is only made for the Italian market – who knows why?

So where did this TEN YEAR myth come from? Ten was a good number to measure by years ago, but with new technology and more savvy whisky makers, whisky can be good at as young as four. Whisky must be aged in a cask for three years by law and maturing time can be determined by a multitude of issues: great casks, whisky making experience and, of course, the terroir.

For example, most writers in the early days of the Arran distillery quoted that the malt was two years ahead of normal due to the warmer climate on the island. Therefore, many single malts under 10 years old are extremely quaffable.

## HERE ARE SOME HELPFUL HINTS WHEN
## READING SINGLE MALT WHISKY LABELS

☐ The first things to look for are the words "Scotch whisky," spelled exactly in that way. If the word Scotch is missing, the whisky is probably made elsewhere. If it says "Scotch Whiskey" or "Scottish Whiskey" it is possibly counterfeit.

☐ Now, look for the words "single malt." This phrase may be split by other words – e.g. single highland malt. If this is present, you have a single malt Scotch whisky. If you have vatted malt or pure malt, you have a mixture of single malt whiskies. Very rarely, you might find a single grain whisky. In all other cases, you have a blended whisky.

☐ The label might identify a distillery name, either as the main brand or as part of the product description. This is not guaranteed for any type of Scotch, but is most likely seen in a single malt. This is no guide to quality, but may mean that successive bottles are completely different whiskies.

☐ In most countries you will see the alcoholic strength. Note the difference between percentage (percentage alcohol by volume) and proof, a measure that varies by country. Typically whisky is around 40% Abv; lower values may be required in some countries, or might indicate an "economy" whisky.

☐ Alcoholic proof is a measure of how much ethanol is in an alcoholic beverage, and is approximately twice the percentage of alcohol by volume (Abv).

The other information that might be present is an age. If an age like 12 years is present that indicates that all the whisky in the bottle was matured in cask at least that long before bottling. You might also see a year. Years are trickier, because whisky stops maturing once it is bottled; examine the labels for the year of bottling. Basic whisky would not include an age, but it is often used to differentiate brands, since more mature whisky may be better and is almost invariably more expensive.

**Chapter**

**11**

# Independent Bottlers (IB's)

I have to say that, in Canada, product from an Independent Bottler (IB) is just not working. There is so much misconception around Independent Bottlers that even people I know with good knowledge of whisky have the totally wrong idea when it comes to IB's. "This is the crap whisky the distilleries did not want," they often say.

This is the first misconception. I must admit, for a young market, IB's should offer just the mothballed or closed distilleries until such time the market becomes educated. Without proper education for the consumer and retailer, these can become far too confusing.

For example, one could see a Highland Park 21 from an IB sitting next to a Highland Park 18 from the actual distillery. Already the consumer is confused. You would automatically assume that both bottles come from the same distillery. Alas! This is not always the case. The Highland Park 21 comes from an Independent Bottler.

Why would a distillery sell their malts to an IB instead of selling it themselves? Simply put, single malts have grown in popularity. When demand goes up so does production. At one time when a distillery met its production before the end of the year they would continue production and sell the whisky to other larger distilleries for blending brokers or to independent bottlers directly. One of the reasons for doing this was to keep the distillery open all year, thereby avoiding employee layoffs. In the USA, the independent bottlers were pioneers and helped to put the interest back into single malts. Many drams were just not available and these companies filled a niche. It seemed that US consumers appreciated the opportunity to drink such rare malts.

The main issue to bear in mind is that when the independent bottlers buy a cask well before the end of maturation they can move this cask to their own warehouse to mature and could even finish it in a different cask. The mistake that many make is assuming that if it tastes different than the distillery's whisky, it is inferior. This is not the case: it may just be different.

These guys aren't dummies. They have spent many years in the whisky industry, some for over 50 years. The IBs don't just buy anything. Similarly, they aren't there to pick out the best from a bunch of casks in a corner that the distillery manager has disregarded. These guys know what they are doing when they are buying casks. For example, the knowledgeable independent bottlers buy the inventory of distilleries that were mothballed or were on their way to being a part of a blend. Without the Independent Bottlers many distillery offerings would no longer be available to the consumer. These IB's often know in advance when a distillery will be mothballed or closed and will quickly buy up the available inventory.

The independent bottlers will nose the casks available, which are probably in production order. Often they buy the casks at an early stage of maturation so they can be matured in their own warehouse. By nosing at regular intervals they may wish to finish the whisky in a different cask, (port for example) and then will determine the age to bottle. Cask strength is again popular and many are bottled this way with no coloring or chillfiltering.

You may see a rare mothballed distillery like Rosebank at your local liquor store. Rosebank is a Lowland treat that you may never have the chance to experience again. You will clearly see on the label this is a IBs expression. The question is, after reading my book, are you ready to take the journey to purchase this Rosebank knowing full well it may not be quite as the exact taste profile of a single malt from the distillery? My suggestion definitely is to try it. It will have the flowers, grassy and citrus fruits associated with a fine Lowland however, depending on age, other tastes and aromas may appear. The distillery was mothballed in 1993 and will probably not reappear.

So when you are at your local liquor store and you see two different Macallan 25 Year Olds, check the two labels carefully. One may be bottled through the distillery and the other bottled at an Independent Bottler's. Remember, the IB's bottling will not have quite the same characteristics as the distillery offering.

Whisky is a journey and it takes considerable time and knowledge to develop your own particular tastes. That's the fun of it!

## Independent Bottlers of Scotland

- ☐ Aberdeen Distillers
- ☐ Douglas Laing & Co. Ltd.
- ☐ Heart Brothers Ltd.
- ☐ Iain Mackillop and Co. Ltd.
- ☐ James MacArthur & Co. Ltd.
- ☐ Murray McDavid
- ☐ Signatory Vintage Scotch Whisky
- ☐ The Vintage Malt Whisky Co.
- ☐ WM Cadenhead Ltd.
- ☐ Blackadder
- ☐ Gordon & MacPhail
- ☐ Hunter Hamilton Company
- ☐ Ian Macleod & Co Ltd.
- ☐ McGibbon's Provenance
- ☐ Robert Scott & Co.
- ☐ The Ultimate Whisky Company
- ☐ Versailles
- ☐ Whisky Galore Ltd.

## Chapter
## 12

# Nose & Taste – The Best Part

Eventually, you may say, "knowledge is power but I really need to drink some of this stuff NOW." You can drink it however you like as long as you pay attention to what makes you feel good. Here I will just offer some tips to get the very best out of your chosen wee dram.

"Keep it very still; what are you doing? Pour it evenly out of the bottle! You have put it into shock! Swirl like the wine drinkers. No never swirl! Don't add water. You must add a splash of spring water. Add lots! At least 50%! Ice cubes are the worst thing you could possibly do – now you have killed it."

Baffled yet? The following debates not only come from books, I have also heard them from some of the top industry experts.

## POUR YOUR DRAM....

Many will say be gentle when pouring it and certainly do not swirl it once it is in your glass. The reasoning behind this would be that the alcohol content at 40% or more will hit your nose like an express train. Keeping the glass and the contents still will make nosing easier.

## TEARS & LEGS....

Tilt the glass 45 degrees and turn the glass very slowly in your fingers for about 30 seconds. Look for the coating on the inside of the glass, known as "tears & legs." Here you are looking to identify the age by watching the tears turn into legs and determining how far apart they are from each other.

The younger the whisky, the faster they will appear and then run down the glass quite close together. Legs of older malts will take time to appear and slide down the glass slowly and further apart.

## COLOUR....

Looking at colour would be the next logical step. I must say, though, it's a crapshoot. Sure there are books out there that tell you how to impress your friends by waxing on about the colour. "Well ladies and gents you can see by the golden colour it has been aged in sherry casks." Very impressive. Yet without doing your homework, how would you know if caramel was added?

What if the distillery reassembled using staves from both casks – smell will often give that away and yet we are still on appearance! So colour is too much guesswork and the reason we have a wee dram in our hand is to drink it!

## NOSE....

Nosing is so overrated in my opinion for the likes of you and me. In the whisky industry distillery managers, stillmen and blenders just use nosing to determine the final product. That takes eons of experience.

The distillery managers rarely taste except in the bar after a hard day at the distillery. Could you imagine tasting a couple of hundred whiskies every day? A trained nose is everything and can detect the slightest impurity or a cask that is just not up to snuff (no pun intended). The spirit is watered down to 20% in order to detect all the available smells.

Nosing is more about the journey as those aromas send you off in a daydream: frolicking in the heather, feeling the salt spray as you approach Islay for a few days of sampling.

One of our whisky club members is a dab hand at nosing and comes up with aromas we would never imagine, whether it is single malts or wine. She once described prunes on a South African Shiraz which none of us had detected until she mentioned it. Her approach is to take a sniff and imagine her life's experiences, particularly as a child.

Begin with three or four sniffs with your whisky neat. The first sniff will be too much and more sniffs will acclimatize your nose to the powerful alcohol. Next, add a gentle splash of spring water and repeat nosing.

Imagine being in your garden on a spring day when the first soft shower arrives. The flowers will begin to open and spread an enchanting variety of aromas. This is what you have done to your malt.

## TASTE....

With the first taste take a generous sip and roll the liquid around all of your mouth and tongue in a chewing fashion. To continue detecting further tastes add drops of water and you will detect more tastes coming through.

Always add water but not a lot. For single malts and vatted/pure malts it's a must. You need it for both nose and taste. In the industry they nose at 20% of the regular alcoholic strength, which, in most cases, is half and half. Malts have oils and ester compounds that cannot appear without water.

Too much water will take away some of the mouthfeel identity; however, more taste may come through. At the end of the day it's your own personal choice. Have I said, "Add water" enough yet?

The old story from Scotland is that the big sissy drinkers south of Hadrian's wall (i.e. me, being from Yorkshire) and those across the pond wanted malts to be at 40% rather than cask strength. Actually, this reduction of alcohol strength was put into effect during the First World War for rationing purposes. Why did it become trendy to stick with these less powerful malts after the war? It may have been that we drinkers prefer to enjoy our whisky rather than in the style of the old western movies. The cowboys would belly up to the salon bar, order a whisky and throw it straight down their throat in one easy motion to avoid burning their mouths!

Whisky, in particular single malts, needs to attract more people: especially the younger crowd fresh out of college. If they have spent their teenage days drinking beer and vodka the last thing they need or appreciate is a fiery spirit. Trust me – add water for both smoothness and taste.

I describe mouthfeel throughout this book based on thickness much like a wine. Most whisky writers use mouthfeel more in describing the taste complexity. Bruichladdich malts, for example, have a thick mouthfeel like cream as opposed to milk, which you can really chew on. This creates a pleasing sensation on your tongue and as it slowly slides down your throat regardless of whether they are a 10 or 17 year old. In most cases the texture comes down to the still. Small, dumpy stills produce a bigger mouthfeel or heavy/oily texture, while the longer stills produce lighter malts. The one exception to that rule is Bruichladdich who are a bit unique in many different ways.

Many times, I am asked by a consumer to give advice on a new malt. Certainly they are leery to spend the money when they aren't confident of their knowledge. This basic shopping guide will help you to choose a new malt that is suitable to your palate.

Remember that you can only detect four predominate tastes with your tongue: salt, sweet, bitter and sour but with your nose you can detect thousands of scents. The following guide will help you understand the various tastes associated with single malts.

## TOP TASTES

*Fruity: Fresh or dried fruits.*

*Citrus: Oranges, lemons, tangerines and limes.*

*Toffee: The sweetest part of the, includes butterscotch.*

*Malty: Breakfast cereal, malted milk. This particular taste comes from the malted barley.*

*Smokey: The wood – pine, oak, tobacco and all that smoke.*

*Peaty: Of course from all those lovely phenols. Includes iodine and will have smokey characteristics.*

*Nutty: All types of nuts and oh, my favourite, – marzipan (ground almonds).*

*Spicy: Ginger, cloves and cinnamon.*

*Sherry: Often included with fruity. I have listed sherry separate to give you a heads up on the different casks used. Often described as sweet on the aftertaste.*

*Vanilla: A usual characteristic from a bourbon cask. Usually grouped with toffee.*

*Oily and Flowery: These two make up the basic flavours before a journey into 500 more, according to some writers. I have purposely omitted these two from our base taste list. After much pondering, I decided who likes to taste oil even with a bunch of flowers? Really both are important and are evident from the casks in maturation. However, the oil taste is all about the texture while the flowery "taste" is mainly an aroma.*

*Feinty: This is an essential taste yet very difficult to detect. It starts in the spirit–run, middle cut as a toasty aroma, detected possibly in the taste as honey.*

*Salty: The big debate continues. Scientists have proved we cannot taste actual salt (well not like the salt we have with vinegar on our fish and chips). Still, you cannot argue with the top whisky writers – well, actually, you can and some do on a regular basis. My colleagues and I certainly taste a maritime flavour of seaweed and salt spray on many Islay & island or coastal single malts.*

While the scientists say organic compounds are responsible, there is the location to be taken into consideration. An example of this is the location of the malting house and warehouse full of maturing casks. Being an island or on the coast, the malting house and warehouse would be continually surrounded by sea spray which contains salt. The main malting houses mentioned earlier are near the sea and most island malts reviewed have salty flavour detected by a wide range of experts.

Another mystery in the fascinating world of whisky!

## Chapter 13

# Whisky & Cheese – Yes Please!

I can just see the Scots reading this and thinking I am proper daft. After all, whisky goes with every thing in Scotland so long as it's a cheap blend totally drowned in water. A fine single malt is to be savored with nothing, nada, noucht.

Britain is well known for its bland traditional food. I agree that a fine single malt would not match particularly well with such foods as shepherd's pie or fish and chips. "Like chalk and cheese," so the expression goes. Speaking of which (what a segue), and this will blow you away, – cheese matches whisky better than wine.

I really don't know how the wine match ever took off as often the cheese will clash. Have you ever sat down with a variety of cheeses and wine and really found good partners? I believe that the match comes from what accompanies the cheeses. If you had fruit such as grapes or pineapple and nuts along with cheese it is probably the fruit rather than the cheese that works well together.

Be daring – there are lots of malts and cheeses out there just waiting to be enjoyed. A great way to experiment is to invite friends around for an evening of sampling both whisky and cheese. You will be pleasantly surprised with the outcome. The more you practice, the more perfect the balances you will find. Many malts can find a cheese partner but some cheeses matches do stink (well, not literally).

Gouda and Muenster lack any kind of punch and Italian Provolone, while having character, is just odd and does not want to play ball. There are 700 cheese varieties available in the UK alone and probably at least that many in Canada and the United States. With this new knowledge you're on your own with matching them all!

I have listed a few basic matches that will give you an idea on how to create your own individual formula. If you agree with me that Wensleydale with blueberries is a perfect match for The Balvenie, then you might want to try your own favourite Speysider.

## MILD CHEESES

Edam Cheese is usually consumed young, when the texture is elastic and supple and the flavour is smooth, sweet and nutty. It is made with part skim milk and has a pale yellow interior and a red wax exterior.

Edam originated in Holland over 800 years ago and the name comes from a town of the same name in southern Holland. Initially, cheese makers shaped Edam into balls to roll down the gangplanks into ships for export.

Gouda comes from the same valley where Edam originated. It is made with whole milk and has a light, buttery, nutty, slightly sweet flavour. The texture is smooth and creamy. Like Edam, it is pale yellow with a coating of red wax.

Note: The use of red wax suggests mild cheese, yellow or clear wax suggests aged or flavoured cheese, and black wax or a brown rind suggests smoked.

Gruyere: Since the 11th century, cheese makers in the Alpine area between Switzerland and France have produced Gruyere. The pride and joy of the region, this cheese received its name from the town of Gruyeres. It is nutty and rich with full bodied flavor. Gruyere cheese is wonderfully complex – at first bite it is slightly fruity, then more earthy and nutty flavours emerge.

The Malts: Glenkinchie, Arran Malt, and Bruichladdich 10 match really well. The Lowland Glenkinchie has a light, flowery style and honey taste. Arran Malt is quite buttery and Bruichladdich has a big mouthfeel yet is gentle on the taste.

## SOFT CHEESES

Softer cheese such as Brie and Camembert require a bit more work. Due to its texture, this type of cheese clings to your mouth and needs either a lighter malt or a fiery, young whisky that does not hang around too long in the finish. I have found that many Non–Chillfiltered whiskies such as Arran NCF are a very pleasant match

The flavours of Brie and Camembert are rich with an earthy, mushroom flavour which changes from mild when young to pungent with age. It is the colour of pale ivory and its texture is creamy and soft with a snowy white, edible rind.

It is important to check the ammonia levels in both these cheeses. Bear in mind, that with their mouth coating texture these cheeses will need a whisky that will temper their lactic acid. I find the lighter malts match well with the softer cheeses; your pallet will be cleansed creating a symphony of tastes.

## HARD CHEESES

The superstar is Dubliner Cheese. This cheese from Ireland is a star choice for single malts. It works tremendously well with Tyrconnell Irish Single Malt (this is definitely a coincidence and quite uncanny).

Normally, I would say to those that suggest matching the country with cheese is rubbish. Actually it's not the country that matches these two, it is the sweet aftertaste of Dubliner the matches the fruity, smooth style of Tyrconnell. Longmorn 15 is another single malt that goes well with this cheese. The friendliest and most versatile cheese for a wide selection of malts is Dubliner.

Cheshire: This cheese is quite firm in texture and a bit more crumbly than cheddar. It is rich, mellow and slightly salty with an excellent aftertaste. Cheshire proved not to be the easiest of matches. Peated malts are too much and the Speysiders are not enough. A big mouthfeel creamy dram such as Bruichladdich is required with just enough humph to balance with the cheese. Other whiskies with a big mouthfeel would be Glenfarclas and Deanston.

Stilton, the "King of Cheese," is a blue mould cheese with a rich and mellow flavor and a spicy aftertaste. Blue cheeses are a perfect match for peaty malts. Here is a selection to keep you going for awhile: Bowmore, Ardbeg, Lagavulin, Laphroaig, Springbank 15 and all those other peaty monsters.

That covers some of the basic cheese types. To experiment even further, try the new fruit and herb cheeses recently introduced. Leading the charge is Wensleydale, and to a lad from Yorkshire, this is the best cheese in the world and now popular due to the Wallace and Gromet series.

Wensleydale with blueberries is quite sweet and the "piéce de la resistance" is Speysiders. I initially tried Old Pulteney – not a Speysider yet quite nice, as well as Tomintoul 10. I then tried Macallan Fine Oak 10 – the match is out of this world when served with any Wensleydale and fruit combinations (Wensleydale and cranberries or apricots).

I found that most cheeses that contain fruit work with single malts. However, I experimented with several herb cheeses such as a welsh cheese with parley and horseradish – and it would not match anything, not even the Lowland malts.

Finally, Non Chillfiltered (NCF) whiskies contain acids and esters; therefore they can breakthrough any cheese that is also high in acids. Cheese contains lactic acid which helps generate flavours during ripening and helps preserve the cheese.

Hard, grating Italian cheese such as Parmesan, Romano and Asiago, provides complex flavour profiles ranging from aromatic dairy to sweet and nutty and finally a savoury background note. Additionally, the Romano type cheeses also deliver bold, sharp and piquant background notes.

It is my recommendation that most of the time you should match strong for strong (flavour for flavour) and occasionally with a cheese such as brie, acid for acid. Aged cheeses really need a single malt with depth or peaty characteristics.

For those who are lactose intolerant goat cheeses will work just fine. Use the same formula and just bear in mind the basics found in this chapter.

(See Table "B" for Single Malts and Cheese matching.)

## Chapter 14

# Islay & Island Distillery Profiles

Keeping in the theme of "Whisky Today," the following is a showcase of the whisky distilleries of Islay & the Islands. These areas of Scotland will continue to produce innovative modern malts and will prove to be the most exciting single malt category for many more years to come.

Every year my grandparents traveled to the Scottish Isles for their holidays – one of their favourite places to vacation. They drove an Austin A35 (small car) and loved to tour around the islands of Scotland. Upon their return, Granddad would fill me with stories about islands with palm trees and white sandy beaches and regale me with the fascinating history of these magical isles. In school, I became a bit of a geography buff and could reflect back on his stories.

Many years later (March 2004), I find myself on the ferry heading to the Isle of Arran which was one of their favourite destinations that boasted palm trees and sandy beaches. Immediately upon leaving the port, although the day is quite overcast, Arran's horizon comes into view – it resembles a great sleeping knight. The outline of the mountains to the north takes on the shape of his helmet. The middle of the island, which is more rolling hills than mountains, shows the knight with his hands folded on his stomach. The lower–lying part of the islands resembles his legs and boots. I then see a pair of golden eagles soaring in the thermals above the island and realize that I am about to land somewhere magical.

The islands of Scotland are called Scotland's other offshore asset as they are one of the most enchanting places on earth. Even the tiniest of these islands has its own individual character and charm. You will find breathtaking scenery, dramatic sunsets, tiny picturesque harbours and abundant wildlife. Islanders are truly a unique set of people – independent and a little mysterious due to their historical roots. Their common thread is community and, of course, when making single malts, a unique terroir.

It's all happening on the Scottish isles. In the last decade, Islay began to see major changes in the world of whisky. Arran Distillery was the first new island pioneer, opening their distillery in 1995. In 1997, Ardbeg was resurrected by Glenmorangie followed by the founding of Bruichladdich – just in time to see the new millennium. Blackwood Distillery, located on the remote Shetlands Islands, is almost ready to introduce their selection of single malts.

Scottish islands are the best places in the world for producing malt whisky. Names such as Laphroaig, Talisker and Highland Park are among the most revered and among the most successful in the whisky world. Market forces, the vagaries of Scottish weather, and the complex logistics of ferrying raw materials to tiny harbours and nursing precious casks over to bottling plants on the mainland.

And what about Islay? The whisky renaissance has re opened two of its great old distilleries. Ardbeg, smoky giant of malts, is back in production for global leader Glenmorangie (LVMH). On the other side of the island, the Bruichladdich distillery has been resurrected by five private individuals – with a little help from their friends, and their bank. Bruichladdich is something of an enigma. Even the pronunciation of its name is controversial: is it brew–ich– laddie or brewy–laddie?

Its whisky is distinctive, with a taste unlike other Islay malts owing to the delicately peated barley used and the exceptionally tall–necked stills that combine to make a sophisticated, elegant, non–medicinal dram bottled at 46% at the distillery, caramel free and without chillfiltration.

Since its rebirth in 2001 as the only privately owned Islay distillery, the fiercely independent Bruichladdich Distillery Company has distinguished itself in many ways. It immediately won a Distillery of the Year award and now has opened a bottling plant which allows whisky to be distilled, matured and bottled on Islay for the first time. It has formed a partnership with a local disability action group to employ disabled workers and welcomes disabled visitors at the distillery. It allows investors to fill their own cask by arrangement, a very personal touch.

The distillery has become a hub for the local community, much as it must have been in the past. Most importantly for whisky lovers, Bruichladdich plans two other malts: the revival of the historic Port Charlotte malt, a peatier cousin of Bruichladdich using the same water, will be accompanied by the creation of a new super malt named Octomore which is to contain twice as much peat as today's heavily peated whisky. Of course, the lighter Bruichladdich malt will continue to be produced using traditional methods and ingredients.

The values of independence and innovation along with community partnerships are revitalizing island malt whisky. Grandeur and tradition (and a wee bit of tartan) are still important, but the future is looking more down– to– earth  and a lot peatier.

## ISLAY

Islay is the most southerly of the Hebrides and is known for its rich and colourful landscape that has been shaped by natural forces and human influence which spans thousands of years.

The farmland, woodland and peat land set below the sweeping hills support a wide variety of wildlife and many bird species, including the rare corncrake. Each autumn the island witnesses clouds of geese arriving to winter on the mild pastures, with Loch Gruinart in the north as the island's main reserve.

Islay is popular with whisky enthusiasts all over the globe, as it is the only Scottish island where you will find seven whisky distilleries. Each one has its own process and unique appeal which makes them well worth a visit. Islay's whiskies are in a category of their own right due to the pungent, concentrated and peaty earthiness of the traditional style of whisky produced.

Tasters speak of seashore and even medicinal dimensions to the richness of the prevailing character yet the whiskies have their own remarkable structure and balance. Despite its peculiarity, traditional Islay whisky is becoming very popular outside Scotland, although some distillers are choosing to lighten the style.

## HOW TO GET THERE

*By Ferry:* Islay can be reached by ferry from Kennacraig, on the Kintyre Peninsula. The Caledonian Macbrayne Ferry takes just over 2 hours. Full details including online booking for both winter and summer ferries are available at www.calmac.co.uk.

If you are using your own boat, Port Ellen has recently had fully serviced pontoons installed for visiting yachts. Other moorings are available at Port Askaig.

*Motorists:* Make sure you fill up with auto fuel on the mainland (at Tarbet or Lochgilphead). Fuel prices are very high on the island.

*By Coach:* CityLink runs a coach service from Glasgow which links with the ferry service.

*By Air:* Islay is twenty minutes flying time from Glasgow and has connections to the rest of Europe and the world.

# ISLAY'S WHISKY DISTILLERIES
# THE LOCH INDAAL DISTILLERIES

The two malts produced on the shores of the loch tend to be less strongly flavoured than their southern cousins, but are still extremely impressive.

## BOWMORE DISTILLERY

Bowmore is the oldest distillery on Islay and dominates the seaward end of the village of Bowmore in the same way the village's round church dominates the landward end.

Their product is one of the best balanced of the Islay distilleries, guaranteed to appeal to a wide variety of tastes. Bowmore distillery was awarded 'The Distiller of the Year Award' by the International Spirits Challenge 2000.

## THEIR WHISKIES:

The spirit that flows through its stills is one of the most lightly peated of the Islay whiskies, despite using malt with a phenol content of over 20 parts per million. The spirit can stand up well to lengthy maturation in rich sherry casks – the highly sought after Black Bowmore is the perfect example of this. The general character of their whiskies is smoky and salty with a slightly perfumed character.

## TOURS:

- ☐ The distillery is open year round, Monday to Friday.

- ☐ Summer tour frequency: 10.30am, 11.30am, 2pm and 3pm. Saturday: 10.30am.

- ☐ Winter tour frequency: 10.30am and 2.30pm.

- ☐ Directions: If traveling down Main Street, make a left at the bottom of the hill before you reach the sea.

- ☐ Groups: Prebooking only with a maximum of 15 per tour group.

- ☐ Cost £2, seniors £1, redeemable in the shop. Under 18 are free.

- ☐ Photography is allowed in the distillery.

- ☐ Disabled access: Designated disabled parking spaces. This tour is ideal for the disabled visitor – flat or gentle slope except for a few steps to the maltings and the hospitality room. In each case there are willing hands to overcome these obstacles. Blind visitors get a great welcome here.

- ☐ Foreign Visitors: Some guides speak foreign languages.

WEBSITE: www.bowmore.com

CONTACT: 44 (0)1496 810671

## BRUICHLADDICH DISTILLERY

Pronounced "brook–laddie," this distillery sits close to Port Charlotte on Islay. Apart from a break in the 1920s and 1930s, whisky has been produced steadily until 1983 when production ceased. In 1985, the future looked bleak as the distillery's owners, Invergordon, were taken over by Whyte and Mackay. They chose to focus efforts on their flagship single malts, Dalmore and Isle of Jura at the expense of Bruichladdich.

In December 2000, all this changed when the distillery was purchased by Mark Reynier and his two Murray McDavid colleagues, Simon Coughlinand & Gordon Wright for £7.5 million. Jim McEwan, the production director, and his team have breathed life back into the place, with Islay's first bottling hall now installed.

### THEIR WHISKIES:

All of Bruichladdich whiskies are bottled where they are distilled. They are matured beside the Atlantic Ocean for freshness and nothing is added but pure, Islay spring water to reduce the cask strength to 46%. Nothing is taken away – all their whiskies are Non–Chillfiltered and are free of colouring. Unpeated barley gives the floral character to the whisky. Distilled on Victorian machinery and tall, narrow necked stills that provide a medicine free, medium–weight body. American oak casks introduce vanilla notes. It is naturally bottled for maximum flavour and rich texture.

## TOURS:

- ☐ Summer tour frequency (Easter to October): Monday to Saturday – 10.30am, 11.30am and 2.30pm.

- ☐ Winter tour frequency (November to Easter): Monday to Saturday – 10.30am and 2.30pm.

- ☐ Directions: If you are already on Islay – Bruichladdich is on the Rhinns peninsula, six miles down the Portnahaven road. There is also regular bus service from Port Askaig, Port Ellen and Bowmore.

- ☐ Groups: Pre Bookingonly, maximum 15.

- ☐ Cruise Ship Access: yes, via Bruichladdich Pier, by arrangement.

- ☐ Cost: £3

- ☐ Photography is allowed in the distillery.

- ☐ Disabled access: Excellent facilities for the disabled.

- ☐ Foreign Visitors: French spoken – by appointment.


WEBSITE: www.bruichladdich.com

CONTACT: 44 (0)1496 850 190

## THE SOUTH COAST DISTILLERIES

The road from Port Ellen signposted to Ardbeg is your key to three of the islands distilleries:

## LAPHROAIG DISTILLERY

Pronounced "La– froyg" was established in 1826. The distillery stayed in the Johnston family for nearly half a century until in 1954, when Bessie Williamson, a well known figure in the world of whisky, inherited the distillery and managed it until 1972. The distillery belonged to Long John Distillers, Whitbread & Co and finally to Fortune Brands. About 10% of the production is marketed as single malt, the remaining part being sold to blenders to produce, amongst others, Long John, Black Bottle and Islay Mist.

Laphroaig has its own peat source on a bog near Port Ellen airfield. The peat is cut and stacked each April, collected in August for storing and drying before being used during the following distillation season. The pair of stills were installed in 1882 followed by a second pair – exact replicas – in 1923, two more in 1968 and then a single additional spirit still, making seven in all, by 1974.

## THEIR WHISKIES:

Today's Laphroaig is famously peated, using malt of 35ppm phenol levels but tasting like much more. Laphroaig is arguably the most distinctive Islay malt, a pungent, primal, classy spirit that has come to embody not only the traditional style associated with the island but also the smell and earthy impact that the rest of the world regards as the essential persona of Scotch malt whisky.

## TOURS:

- ☐ The distillery is open from September to June, Monday to Thursday.
- ☐ Tour Times: 10:15am and 2.15pm.
- ☐ Directions: From Port Ellen take the Ardbeg Road. Laphroaig Distillery is the first of three distilleries on a lovely coastal road. It is down a short drive on the seaward side.
- ☐ Groups: Pre Booking only.
- ☐ Cost is free.
- ☐ Photography is allowed in the distillery.
- ☐ Disabled access: Not an easy tour for the disabled but help is available.
- ☐ Foreign Visitors: No special provisions for non English speaking visitors.

WEBSITE: www.laphroaig.com

CONTACT: 44 (0) 1496 302418

## LAGAVULIN DISTILLERY

Lagavulin (Laga–voolin) means 'the hollow where the mill is,' and was established in 1816.

This distillery stands near the ruins of Dunyveg Castle. It was from here that 1,000 Islaymen set sail to fight alongside Robert the Bruce at Bannockburn in 1314, and in this bay the MacDonald's maintained their power base as Lords of the Isles until they were finally driven out by the Campbells three centuries later. It is now one of Diageo's flagship "Classic Malts" and is certainly one of the most robust, peaty Islay malts around.

## THEIR WHISKIES:

Lagavulin is truly a superb malt that sums up all that is best in the heavily sea influenced whiskies of the south coast. As whisky writer Jim Murray puts it: 'It is not a malt you simply sip; it devours you. Dry smokiness, with complexity through the phenols.'

Peated malt, slow distillation and long maturation together ensure Lagavulin develops a complex, rich, peaty character. Lagavulin is a spirit which likes to take its time. This whisky has the same broad Islay characteristics as Laphroaig – weight, impact, power, concentration – but the details are different. There is a sweet and spicy dash to the malt with a definite elegance that keeps the complexity in hand.

## TOURS:

- ☐ The distillery is open all year, Monday – Friday by appointment only.

- ☐ Tour Times: 10am, 11.30am and 2.30pm. Weekend visits can be arranged if employees are available.

- ☐ Directions: From Port Ellen take the Ardbeg road. Lagavulin is the second distillery on your right.

- ☐ Groups: Pre Booking only, maximum of 14.

- ☐ Cost £3.00. Redeemable in the shop.

- ☐ Photography is allowed in the distillery.

- ☐ Disabled access: There is a hoist to reception, the stillroom can be reached with some difficulty but the rest is not practical.

- ☐ Foreign Visitors: Leaflets in Dutch, French, German, Italian, Japanese and Spanish are available.

WEBSITE: Not Available

CONTACT: 44 (0) 1496 302400

## ARDBEG DISTILLERY

This distillery dates back to 1794, but only reopened a couple of years ago after 20 years of closure. The site's water source, Loch Uigeadail, is superb and has had the honour of having a whisky named after it.

Situated on the south coast of Islay, Ardbeg was famous as a hideout for smugglers who had to make themselves scarce after their cache was discovered by the Excise men in the late 18th century.

Until 1976/77 Ardbeg still had its own malting floor but took their heavily peated malt from the Port Ellen maltings. The distillery was mothballed for most of the 1980s until Glenmorangie took control in 1997 and secured its future.

### THEIR WHISKIES:

It is, perhaps, the one of the most peaty malt whisky in the world. Their whiskies are one of the most strikingly smoky and briny of the Islay malts: an acquired taste worth acquiring. A ferociously phenolic dram which retains an impressive finesse, possibly because of high stills and an unusual purifier on the spirit stills. Ardbeg maintains the robust and earthy aromas associated with Islay malts. It is described as having a hefty bite and a rich finish; the flavours detected include peat– smoke, seaweed, sawdust and iodine. Excellent and exciting when young, endlessly complex and stimulating when bottled old. Ardbeg is a mighty malt and increasingly popular with collectors and auctioneers.

## TOURS:

☐ The distillery is open all year by appointment, from Monday to Friday.

☐ Tour Times: 10:30am, 11.30am, 2.30pm and 3.30pm.

☐ Directions: From Port Ellen take the Ardbeg road, past Laphroaig and Lagavulin and turn down when you see Ardbegs silhouette below you to the right.

☐ Groups: maximum group size is 15. Pre Booking is advisable.

☐ Cost: £2.00, redeemable in the shop with any purchase over £15.

☐ Photography is allowed in the distillery.

☐ Disabled access: No facilities.

☐ Foreign Visitors: *Ardbeg – The Jewel of Islay*, a history of Ardbeg, is available in French, German, Spanish and Italian at £5.

WEBSITE: www.ardbeg.com

CONTACT: 44 (0)1496 302244

## THE SOUND OF ISLAY DISTILLERIES

Islay's last two distilleries lie close to Port Askaig, overlooking the Sound of Islay with Jura and its mountains beyond.

## BUNNAHABHAIN DISTILLERY

Bunnahabhain (meaning 'mouth of the river') shares its name with the village that grew up around it. In effect, development of the distillery created a community dependent upon it for employment. In doing so, an entire village emerged, complete with schoolhouse and village hall.

Prior to the building of the distillery, the adjacent area was inhospitable and uninhabited. Bunnahabhain was designed from the start as a high output malt distillery. Built round a courtyard, in a style that resembles a Bordeaux chateau, the distillery today is little changed.

### THEIR WHISKIES:

Bunnahabhain's water is piped from streams in the surrounding hills and is less peaty than might be expected. It is described as being sweeter than the other Islays, with a smooth initial palate and a long, full finish. It is lighter than the Islay style, with a full, round flavour and is a popular after dinner dram.

## TOURS:

☐ The distillery is open from March to October, Monday to Friday 10am – 4pm. The rest of year tours are by appointment only.

☐ Tour Times: 10.30am, 1.30pm and 2.45 pm.

☐ Directions: Take the A846 from Bowmore towards Port Askaig. Turn left immediately after Kellis at the brown signpost for Bunnahabhain. Travel for 4 miles on a single track road. Distance markers on barrel lids indicate the route.

☐ Groups: Pre Booking with a maximum group size of 15.

☐ Cost £2, redeemable in the shop with any purchase over £15.

☐ Photography is allowed in the distillery.

☐ Disabled access: This distillery is not recommended for the disabled. (No facilities available.)

☐ Foreign Visitors: No facilities.

WEBSITE: www.bunnahabhain.com

CONTACT: 44 (0)1496 840646

## CAOL ILA DISTILLERY

Caol Ila (Gaelic for 'the Sound of Islay') was built in 1846 by Hector Henderson – a Glasgow businessman with a keen interest in distilling. Like Bunnahabhain and Bruichladdich, the development of Caol Ila created a community of its own along with the distillery. Without these distilleries, it is likely that there would have been little sustained human interference in these areas at all.

Caol Ila is hidden in a quiet cove near Port Askaig and many consider this locality to be the wildest and most picturesque of the island. Situated on Loch Nam Ban, the site is ideal thanks to the abundant supply of good water. Today, craftsmen have faithfully reproduced six stills from the original design to ensure the distinctive quality of Caol Ila malt whisky.

The stills at Caol Ila look out over a spectacular view across the Sound of Islay to the mountains of Jura, undoubtedly one of the finest views from any distillery. The whisky distilled here promotes flavours of the peat bogs and the salty sea air.

## THEIR WHISKIES:

Caol lla's whiskies are oily and smoky, with a seaside tang. It lost a little of its peppery character, but the whisky's oily body, highly prized by blenders, intensified in the process. For a long time independent bottlers flew the flag of Caol Ila while Diageo merely used it as a filling in Johnnie Walker. In 2002, Caol Ila launched their own range of three commendable bottlings which are excellent. It is medium– bodied with a rounded flavour. Pale in colour with a greenish tinge, this malt has a peaty nose and distinct floral notes. It is described as tasting slightly of seaweed and iodine, lightly medicinal, smoky, salty, and sweet with a dry peppery finish.

## TOURS:

☐ The distillery is open all year by appointment, from Monday to Friday.

☐ Tour Times: 10am, 11.15am, 1.30pm and 2.45pm.

☐ Directions: Take the A846 from Bowmore towards Port Askaig. Before reaching Port Askaig, take the sign posted road on the left. The road down to the distillery is about 1 mile long, single track with passing areas.

☐ Groups: maximum size 15.

☐ Cost £3, redeemable in the shop.

☐ Photography is allowed in the distillery.

☐ Disabled access: Modern and well lit but stairs make it difficult for disabled visitors.

☐ Foreign visitors: leaflets in Dutch, French, German, Italian, Japanese and Spanish.

Website: Not Available

Contact: 44 (0)1496 302760

## ISLE OF ARRAN

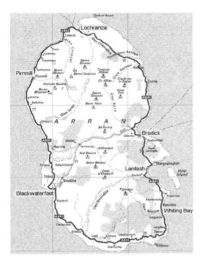

The Isle of Arran is frequently described as 'Scotland in Miniature' due to the beautiful high mountains in the north with gentle rolling hills in the south. Like Scotland itself this magical island, washed by the warm waters of the Gulf Stream, is truly one of nature's gifts. Arran is a small island at 20 miles long and 56 miles round, located off the southwest coast of Scotland.

A beautiful coastline with quaint villages is complemented by a rugged and mountainous interior in the north and green rolling hills and woodland in the south.

Peaceful sandy bays are overlooked by palm trees which grow in the warm climate of The Gulf Stream. The wildlife is exceptional, with deer, pheasant, otter and eagles readily seen in the mountains.

There are colonies of seals near coastal caves, trails and pathways to mysterious Bronze Age Stone Circles, and many relaxing angling hours to be enjoyed by streams or sea.

### HOW TO GET THERE:

The Isle of Arran is within easy reach of Glasgow, making it an ideal holiday destination. Two vehicle ferries run from the Scottish mainland to the Isle of Arran. Most travelers reach the island via Ardrossan which has a direct rail service from Glasgow. These ferries are operated by Caledonian MacBrayne.

## ISLE OF ARRAN DISTILLERY

*'The True Spirit of Nature'*

A dynamic new force in the Scotch whisky industry, Isle of Arran Distillers is one of the few remaining independent distilleries in Scotland. Arran is based at Lochranza on the Isle of Arran, one of the most beautiful and famous islands in Scotland which lies off the west coast between Ayrshire and Kintyre. Early in the 19th century there were more than 50 whisky distilleries on Arran, most of them illegal and carefully hidden from the eyes of the taxmen.

Opened in 1995, the Arran Distillery uses only the traditional methods of distilling, with wooden washbacks and copper stills designed to their exact specification. The Visitor Centre, which was opened in 1997 by Her Majesty the Queen, is built next to the distillery in stunningly beautiful surroundings at Lochranza. Fully guided tours are offered with an audio visual presentation set in a mock eighteenth century Crofter's Inn.

## THEIR WHISKIES:

The location offers perfect water for whisky production and the atmosphere of sea breezes and clear mountain air together with the warm flow of the Gulf Stream matures the Arran Malt to perfection in earth floored warehouses. Arran uses no peat in the production process and no caramel for artificial colouring. Some of their whiskies include Arran Malt, Arran Non–Chillfiltered, Robert Burns Single Malt, Robert Burns Blend, Lochranza Blend and Glen Rosa Blend.

## TOURS:

☐ The distillery is open 7 days a week (April through October) 10am – 6pm (winter hours are reduced).

☐ Tour Times: Every hour on the hour from 10am.

☐ You can also be shown how to 'pour your own' bottle direct from the cask, write your own label and thus enjoy your very own Arran Single Malt to take home.

☐ Directions: Take the Arran Ferry from Ardrossan (in Ayrshire) to Brodick or from Cloanaig (in Kintyre) to Lochranza. The distillery is on the main A841 just north of the Lochranza.

☐ Groups: maximum size 18 (Pre Booking only.).

☐ Cost is £3.50 for adults and £2.50 for students, redeemable in the gift shop.

☐ Photography is allowed in the distillery.

☐ Disabled access: Disabled visitors should enter the parking lot via the smoother entrance on the Lochranza side. Willing hands overcome the obstacle of stairs in the distillery hall.

☐ Foreign visitors: Good leaflets are available in Dutch, Swedish, Portuguese, Japanese, French, German, Italian and Spanish.

WEBSITE: www.arranwhisky.com

CONTACT: 44 (01)770– 830334

## ISLE OF JURA

The Isle of Jura is the third largest of the Islands of Argyll and is dominated by the majestic peaks. Jura is the wildest, emptiest, and least tourist oriented of Britain's inhabited islands. These days the islanders of Jura live on the east coast, where the Jura Distillery is located.

The name "Jura" comes from the Norse words meaning Deer Island. Today over 6500 deer live on six estates on the island. In contrast, the human population is less than 200. From moorland and hills rich in wildlife, to trout–filled lochs, small woodlands, silver sand beaches and rocky shoreline with raised beaches and caves, the island has a lot to offer in the way of landscape.

The island is 29 miles long and 7 miles wide in places. The west is wild and virtually uninhabited, occupied only by the three Paps of Jura which are known in Gaelic as The Mountain of the Sound, The Mountain of Gold and The Sacred Mountain.

Jura's only road leads up the east coast. If you want to get away from it all, this is the place to come. The novelist George Orwell who stayed on the island during the 1940s quite rightly described it as "an extremely un– gettable place."

## HOW TO GET THERE:

*By Bus:* Scottish Citylink buses operate from Glasgow three times per day making a connection with the ferry at Kennacraig.

*By Air:* There is a daily (except Sundays) British Airways service from Glasgow Airport to Islay. The journey then continues by bus or taxi and ferry to Jura.

*By Car:* From Glasgow take the A82 up Loch Lomondside, turn onto the A83 at Tarbet and continue through Inveraray and Lochgilphead towards Tarbert on Loch Fyne. Kennacraig ferry port is about five miles on from Tarbert. The journey takes around two and one half hours.

*By Ferry:* A two hour ferry crossing operated by Caledonian MacBrayne runs from Kennacraig to Port Ellen on Islay. It runs twice daily throughout the year, once on Sundays, with some additional summer season sailings. The ferry crossing from Port Askaig on Islay to Feolin on Jura takes five minutes. Ferries run regularly throughout the day.

## ISLE of JURA DISTILLERY

Jura's single distillery was founded around 1810 and was rebuilt in 1876 but closed during the First World War.

Though a couple of buildings dating back to its early days are still in use, the present distillery was built during the late 1950s and early 1960s and enlarged in the 1970s. It gets its water from a spring called the Bhaille Mharghaidh which flows over rock and carries very little peat. The two pairs of stills are amongst the tallest in the industry, a factor contributing to a light and pure spirit. The wash and spirit stills are very much the same size and are heated internally by steam filled coils.

## THEIR WHISKIES:

Isle of Jura is a light, subtle and intriguing malt whisky. Their whiskies include: Isle of Jura 10 Year Old Single Malt Whisky, Isle of Jura 16 Year Old Single Malt Whisky, Isle of Jura 21 Year Old Single Malt Whisky, Isle of Jura "Superstition" Single Malt Whisky, Isle of Jura Malt Scotch Whisky 1984.

## TOURS:

- ☐ The distillery is open year round by appointment only.

- ☐ Monday – Thursday 9am to 4pm, Fridays 9am to 1pm.

- ☐ Tour Times: 10am, 2pm or by agreement.

- ☐ Directions: From Port Askaig, Islay takes the Ferry to Feolin across the Sound of Islay. Follow the only single track road for 6 miles to Craighouse.

- ☐ Groups: maximum size 15 (Pre Booking only.).

- ☐ Cost is free with a complimentary dram.

- ☐ Disabled access: The distillery is not designed for disabled visitors but the employees will do all they can to assist – the stillroom and cask filling area are within reach.

- ☐ Foreign visitors: No special facilities.

WEBSITE: www.isleofjura.com

CONTACT: 44 (0)1496– 820240

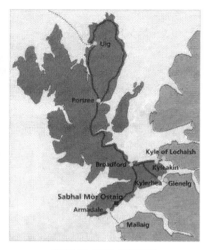

## ISLE OF SKYE

The Isle of Skye is the largest (1,735 sq km), and most northerly island of the Inner Hebrides. Sometimes referred to in Gaelic as Eilean a' Cheò (The Misty Isle), Skye is renown for its natural beauty, history and wildlife.

Skye has an irregular coastline and many of its lochs are rimmed by lofty, sheer precipices. The Cuillin Hills rise to more than 910 metres. Only a small part of the island is arable.

Sheep and cattle raising, wool weaving, whisky distilling, and fishing are the chief industries. The climate is mild and so Skye is a resort despite its heavy rainfall. The Skye Bridge was constructed in 1995, connecting the island to the mainland. Wildlife abounds on the island, with birds from the tiny goldcrest to magnificent golden eagle, mammals from pygmy shrew to red deer and fish from saithe to salmon. If you are lucky, you might catch sight of the elusive otter. The wide range of geology and topography provides habitats for many wildflowers. Gaelic culture and heritage pervade the atmosphere.

## HOW TO GET HERE:

*Skye Bridge:* Kyle to Kyleakin, open 24 hours (no tolls).

*By Ferry:* Cal Mac Ferry: Mallaig to Armadale (a 30 minute crossing) Kylerhea Ferry: Glenelg to Kylerhea (5 minute crossing), Easter to October.

*By Bus:* Citylink: Daily bus service to Broadford, from Inverness and Glasgow. They also run services all over Scotland. Their best prices are found on their own website. Megabus has daily services to Inverness from Perth, Glasgow, Edinburgh and London. Rapsond has local bus service from Broadford.

*By Train:* First Scotrail: Rail service from Inverness to Kyle, Glasgow to Mallaig. A sleeper service runs from London to Inverness and from London to Fort William. GNER: Daily service to Inverness from Edinburgh and London, stopping in many other places between Inverness and London.

*By Air:* Inverness Airport is the closest airport. Timetables and lots of other information can be found on their website.

## TALISKER DISTILLERY

The Isle of Skye is a world of its own and at Talisker, the islands only distillery, even the money was once unique. Distillery workers were once paid in specially minted coins with face values equaling the number of days worked, employees exchanged the coin for the necessities of life, such as herring, oatmeal and flour.

Talisker Distillery was founded in 1830 and since that time has passed through the hands of quite a few including a couple of unscrupulous business men. The reputation of Talisker Single Malt Scotch Whisky as the Golden Spirit of Skye, however, remained undiminished.

The distillery had always imported barley and other supplies while exporting filled casks of whisky in small coasters, known affectionately as "puffers." Along with most other malt distilleries, Talisker was closed between 1941 and 1945 because of government restrictions on the supply of barley to conserve food supplies during the Second World War. Production ceased for a second time when the stillhouse was destroyed by fire in 1960. In a major exercise to conserve the unique flavour of Talisker, the five stills which had been lost in the fire were replaced with exact copies when the distillery reopened in 1962.

## THEIR WHISKIES:

This alluring, sweet, full–bodied spirit is so easy to enjoy, and like Skye itself, so hard to leave.

## TOURS:

- ☐ The distillery is open from Easter to October inclusive, Monday to Saturday, 9:30am to 5pm; November to March, 2 – 5pm.

- ☐ Tour Times: Every ½ hour until 4pm in the summer. The last tour is at 3:30pm in the winter.

- ☐ Directions: Leave the main road to Portree at Sligachan and take the A863 signposted for Dunvegan. After 5 miles, turn left onto the B8009 to Carbost. Follow the distillery signs along this narrow road.

- ☐ Groups: maximum size 16 (Pre Booking only.).

- ☐ Cost £5.00, redeemable in the gift shop. Under 18 – free.

- ☐ Photography in distillery: No.

- ☐ Disabled access: Only to the stillroom floor, warehouse and shop.

- ☐ Leaflets on distilling in Dutch, French, German, Italian, Spanish and Japanese. Handboards in French, German, Italian and Spanish at each stage of the tour.

WEBSITE: UNAVAILABLE

CONTACT: 44 (0)1478 614308

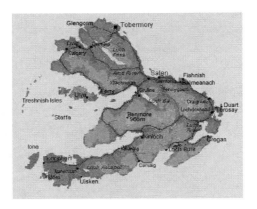

## ISLE OF MULL

This island is approximately 300 square miles in size and is the 3rd largest of the Hebridean archipelago. These are silent, lonely islands of rushing, tumbling burns, high peaks, dramatic views, waterfalls, wildlife, history and atmosphere.

The Isle of Mull has the greatest biodiversity of any place of comparable size in Britain. There are 1,000 foot seacliffs, powdery white sand beaches and a mountain range, with the highest mountain, Ben More, rising 3,000 feet from a very blue and crystal clear sea. The coastline alone covers 300 miles – and yet, there are only 2700 people living in this powerfully beautiful place.

Golden eagles and the very rare white tailed sea eagle have their stronghold here, as does the otter. Dolphins, whales and basking sharks are seen regularly around Mull and the 200 smaller islands and rocky outcrops that surround it.

Tobermory, the capital of Mull, lies toward the northern end of the island. The bay is one of the safest anchorages in the Hebrides. Indeed the original name for the distillery, Ledaig (pronounced Lea–chaig), is Gaelic, and means "safe haven." Thus it was the ideal place for a fishing town which was built here in 1788. The distillery is situated at the southern end of the harbour. These days the main activities on the island are tourism, agriculture, forestry and, of course, distilling. There is not a harbour in Britain to match Tobermory with its famous brightly painted buildings and lively atmosphere.

The name "Tobermory" is derived from the Gaelic "Tobar Mhoire," which means "Well of Mary" relating to the well and chapel of St. Mary. Tobermory Distillery is one of Scotland's oldest operational malt whisky distilleries and celebrated its 200th anniversary in 1998.

## HOW TO GET THERE:

Ferries cross to the island at three points: Oban, Lochaline and Kilchoan and booking is required during busy summer months on the Oban ferry.

The other two ferries are not possible to book, but this usually is not necessary. The Lochaline crossing is a cheaper option and is used regularly by locals.

## TOBERMORY DISTILLERY

Tobermory is the main village on Mull and the home of the distillery. It is dramatically located at the foot of a steep hill and signals the beginning of the village, which spreads around a broad bay.

The distillery was founded in 1798 and the present buildings were erected during its first period of operation which continued until 1826. The distillery was 'silent' for long periods in the mid 1800s and mid 1900s and was twice revived during the 1970s. Now it has been revived again.

### THEIR WHISKIES:

*Tobermory*, which is distilled from unpeated malted barley and allowed to mature in oak casks for a minimum of 10 years, is light amber in colour, with a fresh, lightly peated, smoky nose. The palate is medium dry, smooth and fruity, with a rich and well rounded finish. Tobermory is only lightly peated, drawing its overtones from the water on the Island only. This makes it particularly easy to drink, and is why it serves as the perfect introduction to Island Malt Scotch Whiskies.

*Ledaig*, unlike Tobermory, is distilled from heavily peated malted barley. During the malting process, burning peat is used to dry the barley in a kiln. The reek from the burning peat is absorbed by the barley through the husk of the grain, and remains through the mashing, fermentation and distillation processes, eventually leading to a superior single malt with a highly distinctive peaty, smoky taste.

## TOURS:

☐ The distillery is open from Easter to end of October, Monday to Friday, 10am to 5pm.

☐ Every half hour from 10.30am on.

☐ Directions: From the ferry terminal at Craignure, travel 21 miles on the A849 to Tobermory. After Salien the road is single track and the distillery is on your right as you enter the town.

☐ Groups: maximum size 25 (Pre Booking only.).

☐ Cost £2.50, redeemable in the gift shop.

☐ Photography in distillery: No.

☐ Disabled access: No access – not recommended.

☐ Leaflets in French.

WEBSITE: www.burnstewartdistillers.com

CONTACT: +44 (0)1688 302645

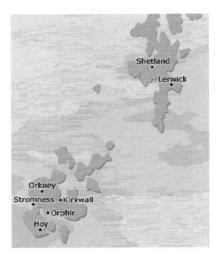

## ORKNEY ISLAND

*Orkney* is made up of 70 or so islands; exact agreement as to the total number of islands is difficult as many are little more than skerries, that is, small uninhabited islets. Of these islands, only 16 are inhabited. Lying on latitude 59 degrees north – which is only 50 miles south of Greenland – Orkney is, at its widest, 30 miles from east to west and 53 miles north to south. With a total coastline of approximately 570 miles, the Orkney Islands cover an area of 974 square kilometers (376 square miles).

The islands are low lying, gently sloping and richly fertile with the exception of the island of Hoy, which is high and rugged. The climate is temperate, warmed by the Gulf Stream; with the driest months being April, May and June. Orkney's is famous for its archaeology, superb wildlife, landscape, and traditional island welcome. Two distilleries remain on the island: Scapa and Highland Park. In general, the whiskies are malty, dry and frequently marked by a spicy/nutmeg/coriander quality.

## HOW TO GET TO ORKNEY ISLAND:

*By air:* British Airways' flights (operated by Loganair) from major British airports and good inbound links from European and North American destinations.

*By land and sea:* Whether you travel by car, coach or train, the main approach follows the A9 from Perth to Caithness. The A9 connects from central Scotland and England's main motorway and rail networks. Dual carriageway connects Aberdeen to central Scotland.

*By car:* From Perth to Inverness is 114 miles through some of Scotland's most beautiful landscape. From Inverness to Scrabster is a spectacular 111 miles.

*By train:* You can travel to Thurso, where a bus connects to the ferry at Scrabster, or Aberdeen, where the station is near to the harbour area. There is also a coach connection from Inverness / Wick to Gills Bay.

*By coach:* You can go either to Scrabster or to John O' Groats (but remember that the John O' Groats route is a summer, passenger– only service).

*Visit Orkney's official visitors' guide to the Orkney Islands*

*Travel, accommodation, attractions, events*

*www.visitorkney.com*

# THE DISTILLERIES OF ORKNEY

## HIGHLAND PARK

Highland Park comes from a land full of mystery that's rich in anecdote and history. Established in 1798 on Orkney, Highland Park is one of the most northerly Scotch whisky distilleries in the world.

Windswept moors and craggy outcrops combined with the wind, rain, lightening, freezing ice, crushing waves and hail provide the perfect setting for Highland Park.

Many of the distillery workers have been there for over twenty years and indeed many follow in the footsteps of their fathers and grandfathers before them. All adhere to traditional methods of distilling that go way back – for at Highland Park, unlike many a distillery these days, no corners are cut.

## THEIR WHISKIES:

In particular, Highland Park continues to malt its own barley using the traditional floor malting method and to kiln dry the 'green' malt using peat cut from its own moorlands. That's why, at Highland Park, you can still see and smell smoke wafting from its pagoda–

style chimneys. Indeed, in the world of single malts, there are few other brands so consistently lauded by connoisseurs and experts alike.

## TOURS:

☐ Summer hours: May to August: Open 7 days. Monday– Friday. Also open April, September and October. Saturday 10am–5pm and Sunday 12–5pm. Tours every half hour, last tour at 4pm.

☐ Winter hours: The distillery is open November to end of March, Monday to Friday. One tour only per day – 2pm.

☐ Directions: From the Stromness on the A964, turn right on the outskirts of Kirkwall at the Esso into Pickquoy Road, then at the T junction, make a right and after a short distance join the A961 for South Ronaldsay. The distillery is on the left.

☐ Groups by appointment only (maximum 15).

☐ Cost £3.00.

☐ Photography in distillery: No.

☐ Disabled access: Excellent access

☐ Audiovisual in English, French, German and Italian. Guides speak Norwegian, French and German. Leaflets in these languages and Japanese.

WEBSITE: www.highlandpark.co.uk

CONTACT: 44(0) 1856 874619

## SCAPA DISTILLERY

Beneath the waters of Scapa Flow still lie the hulks of the German war fleet from World War I, scuttled on the orders of von Reuter who was fed up with the slowness of the post war repatriation negotiations. Scapa was built in 1885 by a Speyside distiller named John Townsend.

It was saved from total destruction by fire during the First World War through the assistance of navel personnel billeted in the area, who arrived by the boatload to help put out the blaze. During World War II, convoys gathered here to be escorted across the Atlantic. Scapa distillery was also used as accommodation for naval ratings.

Scapa was silent for two years from 1934 and was owned for a time by the owners of Glen Scotia Distillery in Campbeltown. The distillery was bought by Hiram Walker in 1954 and rebuilt in 1959, with further internal improvements made in 1978. A major part of the production was used in the Teacher's and Ballantines blends.

## THEIR WHISKY:

Scapa is available as a 12 Year Old bottling. It has a gold color and a light nose, with touches of oak, vanilla, and rich chocolate. The palate is smooth, soft, with creamy and salty notes. The finish is a little salty, slightly peppery, and leaves with a faint buttery echo.

## TOURS:

Conflicting information exists on whether the distillery is open to tourists or not. We are assuming since the recent buy out by Pernod Ricard, that it is closed. Stayed tuned for further information. Our spies tell us that there is something in the works.

Directions: From the Highland Park Distillery it's a small walk to Scapa Beach where you could look around the Scapa Distillery. The distillery site also has a lot of history attached so it is worth the walk.

WEBSITE: NA

CONTACT DISTILLERY OFFICE: 44(0) 1856 872 071

# THE SHETLAND ISLANDS

The Shetland Islands' environment is ideal for making whisky: plenty of water from the sky, plenty of salt spray from the sea, and plenty of rich peat from the earth which has hardly seen commercial exploitation. Water flows up from sandstone and shoots out from springs all over the Shetland Islands before flowing into a burn that meanders over peat and then down to the cove, untouched by humankind from source to sea.

The lochs behind the distillery, fed by the high rainfall in the area, are the source for other processes as they are cooling waters. Due to the extreme northern latitude and cool weather, Shetland peat grows incredibly slow and includes local flora unique to the area. This leads to a rich, aromatic peat ideally suited for whisky production. At 60° North, Shetland is on the same latitude as Alaska or St. Petersburg.

You might expect the weather to be Arctic like in winter, yet it rarely falls below freezing. The Northern Drift, an offshoot of the Gulf Stream, flows rapidly past Shetland. Seed pods from the balmy Caribbean have been known to wash up on the shore. The effect of the Drift is to warm the climate in winter and cool it in summer so that temperatures vary only a little year round (5– 15°C on average). It also rains two days out of every three.

## BLACKWOOD DISTILLERY

Blackwood is by far Scotland's northernmost distillery. The distillery is located in a small cove 10 miles north of Lerwick. The distillery site is at Catfirth, the location of the old RAF base. This is in the South Nesting area on the Mainland of Shetland.

Although still in the production stages, their website states that there are "first indications of a truly great malt." Samples have been made using local peat, water and Scottish barley, replicating the climactic conditions.

The results suggest that the whisky, both peated and unpeated, will have its own unique character distinctive to Shetland itself. The closest references are lightly peated Islay whisky or other outstanding northern malts such as Highland Park on Orkney. We expect different wood finishes will bring out various flavour profiles in both the peated and unpeated malts and indeed show the potential to be accessible in taste as outstanding, easy drinking whiskies.

The same unique features that make Shetland such an ideal place for distilling whisky produce one other distinctive side effect. The sea and the rain make the air so moist that the normal level of 2% per year evaporation of whisky from the barrels into the air is greatly reduced leaving an even richer whisky behind.

## HOW TO GET TO THE SHETLANDS

*By Air:* You can travel via Edinburgh, Glasgow, Inverness or Aberdeen. Less than one hour flying time from Aberdeen, and just over one hour from Edinburgh, Shetland is within easy reach of the UK mainland and connecting routes. Sumburgh Airport is located on the southernmost tip of Shetland. From here, the airport bus to the capital of Lerwick takes around 40 minutes. Hire cars and taxis are available at the airport – booking in advance is advisable.

*By Sea:* The new state of the art NorthLink ships operate daily from Aberdeen. If you are arriving from Scandinavia, or looking for a dual destination holiday, Smyril Line operates regular services to Norway, Iceland, Denmark and Faroe. You will dock at Lerwick Ferry Terminal, only 2 miles from the centre of town. At the terminal, visitor information is available at the Welcome Point in the main concourse.

*www.shetlandwhisky.com & www.blackwooddistillers.com*

*The Shetland Islands official visitors' guide*

*Travel, accommodation, attractions, events*

*www.visitshetland.com*

## Chapter 15

# The Oscars

Now for a little fun! In case you didn't know, many of us in the sales and marketing arena spend endless hours coming up with new ideas to promote our products. Single Malts are no exception with whisky tastings, including trivia questions to win spot prizes, new methods of detecting tastes and even matching with food.

After endless Saturday mornings of watching football (soccer) and pondering in between a shot on goal, I finally came up with something fun and creative that would fit nicely in "Whisky Today." The Oscars! The following is my "hit" list for this year, Oscar–winners in the world of whisky.

*Bruichladdich, Islay: Movie – Cinderella Man (Men).* Boxer James J. Braddock just never gave up in the ring and shocked the boxing world when he eventually became world champion. The Bruichladdich Distillery was out for the count a few times until the year 2000.

*"Four passionate men, a private distillery and a freedom of expression*
*Hand crafting Natural Islay Whisky for the enlightened palate.*
*Scotland's purest, most elegant spirit*
*Distilled on Victorian machinery by Islanders – Natural Born Distillers"*

Since then, they have won numerous prestigious awards and continue to surprise the industry with their innovative ideas while keeping with a time honoured approach. A big peaty monster has now been thrown into the mix.

*Springbank, Campbeltown: Movie – Local Hero.* I had to pick a movie about Scotland. An American oil company sends a man to Scotland to buy up an entire village where they want to build a refinery. But things don't go as expected. The plot of this movie is similar to *Springbank*. This is the oldest independent family run distillery in Scotland: in operation since 1828, it is still run by the Mitchell family. They have stayed with tradition, incorporating the entire production on site. Floor malting, distilling, bottling and the whisky has no chillfiltering or colouring.

*Glenmorangie, Highlands: Movie – The Lord of the Rings.* I chose this movie because it is a big winner in the special effects category. Glenmorangie is the #1 selling single malt in Scotland. Cask finishing seems to work well with their lighter malts that are distilled from the tallest stills in Scotland. Their whisky seems to be the perfect marriage for other imported liquids from casks. The very special effects that result from unique cask finishing keep Glenmorangie in the forefront of innovation.

*The Macallan, Speyside: Movie – Star Trek.* "Space, the final frontier. Her five– year mission: to explore strange new worlds, to seek out new life and new civilizations, to boldly go where no man has gone before." This opening line from *Star Trek* is completely in line with The Macallans quest for the perfect dram. Not only do they still abide by most traditional methods and use only the best barley, they are very innovative when it comes to using a scientific approach in the making of their whisky. They have a first class wood policy: using only new sherry casks where possible. There's nothing wrong with trying to be a perfectionist! – Right Spock?

*Glenfiddich, Speyside: Movie – Lock, Stock and Two Smoking Barrels.* Guy Ritchie made his name when he produced this relatively low–budget film. This is not the best link to Scotland, as this film takes place in East London (complete with the cockney accent); however, Guy and the missus (Madonna) do spend a lot of time in Scotland. This range of malts is a must for drinkers wishing to embark on a journey in single malts. It is an affordable, easy drink and will fit your budget, much like the movie. Glenfiddich still uses traditional methods of distilling and yet manages to produce several million cases per year. They are one of the few distilleries left that use coal to fire their stills and have their own bottling plant.

*Isle of Arran: Movie – Harry Potter (all of 'em).* Both the distillery and the *Harry Potter* series have proved to be two mega hits in the last few years. Arran has just celebrated their 10th anniversary and has proved that their whiskies are some of the finest around. They have had rave reviews after only seven years of maturation for their flagship, Arran Malt, and for the Non–Chillfiltered. The Isle of Arran Distillery is now making a name for themselves with their single cask offerings. These could be finished in port, rum, Premier Grand Cru and even a cask from the cellars of Gianni Masciarelli, one of Italy's premier wine makers. Arran is definitely a pioneering influence on many independently run distilleries today.

*Bladnoch, Lowlands: Movie– Back to the Future.* Bladnoch is the most southerly of Scotland's distilleries. The distillery was founded in the early 1800s, closed in 1938, reopened in the 1950s and then taken over by Bells in 1983 before being mothballed in 1994. In '95, Raymond Armstrong, of Northern Ireland, purchased Bladnoch from United Distillers. The sale went through under the provision that Bladnoch would never produce whisky again. Over the course of the next five years, Armstrong fought to have the restriction removed and finally, in 2000, this was achieved. There is now a bright 'future' to enjoy this true lowland malt once again.

# Savvy Shopping Guide – Table "A"

| Whisky | Peat | Smoky | Salty | Spice | Citrus | Fruity | Malty | Nutty | Honey | Toffee | Vanilla | Sherry |
|---|---|---|---|---|---|---|---|---|---|---|---|---|
| Aberlour 10 | • | | | • | | | | | • | • | | • |
| Ardbeg | • | | • | | | | | | | | | |
| Arran Malt | | | | | • | • | • | | | | • | |
| Arran NCF | | | | • | • | | | | | | | |
| Auchentoshan 10 | | | | | • | | | | | | • | |
| Balblair 16 | | | | • | | | | | | • | | |
| Benriach 10 | | | | | | • | | | | • | | |
| Benromach 12 | | | | • | | | | • | | | | |
| Bowmore 12 | • | | • | | | | | | | | | • |
| Bowmore 17 | • | | • | | | | | | | | | • |
| Bowmore Legacy | • | | • | | | | | | | | | |
| Bruichladdich 10 | | | | | • | • | | | | | • | |
| Bruichladdich 14 | | | | | | • | • | | | | • | |
| Bruichladdich 15 | | | • | • | | | • | • | | | | |
| Bunnahabhain | | | | | | | • | • | | | | • |
| Caol la 15 | • | • | • | | | | | | | | | • |
| Cragganmore 12 | • | | | | | | • | | | | • | |
| Dalmore 12 | | | • | • | • | | | | • | | | • |
| Dalwhinnie 15 | | | | | | | | | • | | | |
| Deanston 12 | | | | | • | | | | • | | | |

| Whisky | Peat | Smoky | Salty | Spice | Citrus | Fruity | Malty | Nutty | Honey | Toffee | Vanilla | Sherry |
|---|---|---|---|---|---|---|---|---|---|---|---|---|
| Edradour 10 | • |  |  | • |  | • | • | • |  |  |  |  |
| Glen Ord |  |  |  |  | • |  |  |  |  |  |  | • |
| Glendronach 12 |  | • |  |  |  |  |  |  |  | • |  |  |
| Glendronach 15 |  |  |  |  |  |  |  | • |  |  |  | • |
| Glenfarclas 15 |  |  |  |  |  |  |  |  |  |  | • | • |
| Glenfiddich 12 |  |  |  |  |  | • |  | • | • |  | • |  |
| Glenfiddich Solera |  |  |  | • |  | • | • |  |  |  |  |  |
| Glenfiddich S Res |  |  |  |  |  | • | • |  |  |  |  |  |
| Glengoyne 10 |  |  |  |  | • | • |  |  | • |  |  |  |
| Glenkinchie 10 |  |  |  |  |  |  | • |  |  |  | • |  |
| Glenlivet 12 | • |  |  | • |  | • |  |  |  |  |  |  |
| Glenlossie 10 |  | • |  |  |  |  |  | • | • |  |  |  |
| Glenmornagie 10 |  |  |  |  |  |  |  | • |  |  |  | • |
| Glenmornagie 15 |  |  |  | • |  | • |  |  |  |  |  |  |
| Glenrothes |  | • |  |  |  |  |  |  |  |  | • |  |
| Highland Park 12 | • | • | • |  | • |  |  | • | • |  |  | • |
| Highland Park 18 |  |  |  |  |  |  |  |  | • |  | • | • |
| Isle of Jura 10 |  | • | • |  |  |  | • |  | • |  |  |  |
| Isle of Jura 16 |  |  |  |  |  |  |  | • |  |  |  | • |
| Jura Superstition |  |  |  |  |  |  | • |  | • | • |  |  |
| Knockando 15 |  |  |  |  |  |  | • | • |  |  |  |  |
| Lagavulin 16 | • |  |  | • |  |  |  |  |  |  |  |  |
| Laphroaig 10 | • |  | • | • |  |  |  |  |  |  |  |  |

| Whisky | Peat | Smoky | Salty | Spice | Citrus | Fruity | Malty | Nutty | Honey | Toffee | Vanilla | Sherry |
|---|---|---|---|---|---|---|---|---|---|---|---|---|
| Littlemilll 8 | | | | • | | | • | | | | | |
| Longmorn 15 | | | | | | • | • | | | | | |
| Mortlach 16 | | • | | • | | | | | | • | | • |
| Oban 14 | | • | • | | | | • | | | | | |
| Old Fettercairn 10 | • | | | | | • | | | | | | |
| Scapa | | | • | | • | | | | | | • | |
| Singleton | | | | | | | | | | • | | • |
| Speyburn 10 | | | | • | | | • | | • | | | |
| Springbank 10 | • | | • | | | | | | | • | | |
| Springbank 15 | • | | • | | | | | | | | | • |
| Strathisla | | • | | | | • | | • | • | | | |
| Talisker 10 | • | • | • | • | | | • | | • | | | |
| *Talisker | • | | | | | | | | | • | | |
| Tamdhu | | • | | • | • | | | | • | | | |
| The Balvenie 10 | | | | | | | | | • | | | • |
| **The Balvenie 12 | | | | | | • | • | • | • | | | • |
| The Macallan 10 | | | | • | | • | • | • | | | | • |
| The Macallan 12 | | • | | • | | • | • | | | | | • |
| *** Macallan 10 | | | | | | • | • | | | | | |
| The Macallan 18 | | | | | | • | | • | | | • | |
| Tomintoul 10 | | | | • | | | | | | | | |
| Tomintoul 16 | | | | • | | • | | | | | | |
| Tullibardine 10 | | | | • | | | | | | • | | |

* Talisker Distillery Addition
** The Balvenie 12 DoubleWood
*** The Macallan 10 Fine Wood

# Matching Single Malts & Cheese – Table "B"

## Recommended Matches

| | | | |
|---|---|---|---|
| Edam/Gruyere | Glenkinchie 10 | Arran Malt | Balvenie 10 Founders |
| Dubliner | Tyrconnell | Longmorn | Bruichladdich 10 |
| Apple Cheddar | Balvenie DW 12 | Highland Park 12 | Glenmornagie 10 |
| Wensleydale & Blueberries | Macallan 10 Fine Oak | Tomintoul 10 | Glenfarclas 15 |
| Danish Blue/Stilton | Ardbeg | Lagavulin | Bruichladdich 3D |
| Stilton/Ginger | Highland Park 18 | Bowmore 17 | Talisker 10 |

## Suggested Matches

| | | | |
|---|---|---|---|
| Edam/Gruyere | Cragganmore 12 | Aberlour 10 | Tullibardine 10 |
| Dubliner | Eradour 10 | Glenfidddich Solera | Macallan 12 YO |
| Apple Cheddar | Dalmore 12 | Deanston 12 | Glengoyne 10 |
| Wensleydale & Blueberries | Isle of Jura 16 | Knockando 1990 | Dalwinnie 15 |
| Danish Blue/Stilton | Laphroaig | Connemara | Springbank 10 |
| Stilton/Ginger | Edradour 10 | Glenlivet 12 | Scapa 12 |

## Chapter
# 16

# Distillery Information

### LIST OF DISTILLERIES & THEIR STATUS

**Operational Distillery:** A distillery which is working and producing spirit or in its silent season. Although such a distillery is maturing the spirit it has produced, it may not have been producing for a sufficient number of years in its present form to be making its whisky available for wholesale or retail.

**Mothballed:** These distilleries are temporarily closed, usually in order to prevent the build up of too much whisky in stock given the trading conditions at the time. Mothballing usually implies some action has been taken to prevent the deterioration of all the buildings and equipment at the distillery. Although such a distillery may not be producing, it could still be maturing stocks in bond.

**Closed Distillery:** A distillery which has been permanently closed down, probably because it was not economical to run at the time of closure. However, there could still be stocks of whisky from such a distillery maturing in bond which would be bottled and sold at the appropriate time, quite probably with the addition of the word "Rare" on their label. When closure happens the equipment is normally dismantled and sold off, so it becomes very unlikely that the distillery could re open in its usual form. The buildings and land can be sold off for other use but this then becomes a lost distillery. While the buildings are still present, one can only hope that the distillery could, in the future, be revived.

**Lost Distillery:** A distillery which has been permanently closed down and its buildings either demolished or converted for other purposes. There might just be a small stock of its whisky still available at a premium if it closed comparatively recently, but stocks in the older lost distilleries will have become exhausted.

## TABLE "C"

## LOST, MOTHBALLED or CLOSED DISTILLERIES

| | | |
|---|---|---|
| Banff | Speyside | Lost 1983 |
| Ben Wyvis | Highlands | Closed 1977 |
| Braeval | Speyside | Closed 2002 |
| Brora Distillery | Highlands | Closed 1983 (Diageo) |
| Caperdonich | Speyside | Closed 2002 (Pernod Ricard) |
| Coleburn Distillery | Speyside | Closed 1992 (license revoked) |
| Convalmore Distillery | Speyside | Closed 1985 (William Grant) |
| Dallas Dhu | Speyside | Closed 1983 (museum) |
| Glen Albyn | Highlands | Lost 1988 |
| Glen Flagler Distillery | Lowlands | Closed 1985 |
| Glen Mhor Distillery | Speyside | Lost 1986 |
| Glen Scotia | Lowlands | Sporadic production |
| Glencadam | Highlands | Closed 2000 |
| Glencraig | Speyside | Closed 1981 |
| Glenesk | Highlands | Closed 1985 (license revoked) |
| Glenglassaugh Distillery | Speyside | Closed 1986 |
| Glenlochy Distillery | Highlands | Closed 1983 |
| Glenugie | Highlands | Lost 1983 |
| Glenury Royal Distillery | Highlands | Lost 1985 (license revoked) |
| Hazelburn | Campbeltown | Closed 1925 |
| Imperial | Speyside | Mothballed 1998 (P. Ricard) |

| | | |
|---|---|---|
| Inverleven Distillery | Lowlands | Closed 1991 |
| Killyloch Distillery | Lowlands | Closed 1985 |
| Kinclaith Distillery | Lowlands | Lost 1976 |
| Ladyburn Distillery | Lowlands | Lost 1976 |
| Littlemill Distillery | Lowlands | Lost 2004 (fire) may open again |
| Lochside | Highlands | Lost 2002 |
| Millburn | Highlands | Lost 1988 |
| North Port / Brechin | Highlands | Closed 1983 |
| Parkmore | Speyside | Closed 1931 |
| Pittyvaich Distillery | Speyside | Mothballed 1993 |
| Port Ellen | Islay | Lost 2003 |
| Rosebank Distillery | Lowlands | Closed 1993 |
| St. Magdalene Distillery | Lowlands | Lost 1983 |
| Tamnavulin | Speyside | Mothballed '96 (W&M) |

# TABLE "D"
# THE REGIONS AND THEIR WHISKIES
## ISLAY

| | |
|---|---|
| Ardbeg | LVMH |
| Bowmore | Suntory |
| Bruichladdich | Bruichladdich |
| Bunnahabhain (F. Grouse) | CL World Brands |
| Caol Ila (Bells & JW Black) | Diageo |
| Lagavulin | Diageo |
| Laphroaig | Fortune Brands |

## ISLE OF ARRAN

| | |
|---|---|
| Isle of Arran | Isle of Arran |

## ISLE OF JURA

| | |
|---|---|
| Jura | Whyte & Mackay |

## ISLE OF MULL

| | |
|---|---|
| Tobermory | CL World Brands |

## THE ORKNEY'S

| | |
|---|---|
| Highland Park (F. Grouse) | Edrington Group |
| Scapa (Ballantines & Teachers) | Pernod Ricard |

## THE SHETLAND ISLANDS

| | |
|---|---|
| Blackwood | Blackwood Distillery |

## CAMPBELTOWN

| | |
|---|---|
| Glen Scotia | Loch Lomond |
| Springbank | J&A Mitchell Co |

# ISLE OF SKYE

Talisker (JW Blk, White Horse)  Diageo

## SPEYSIDE

| | |
|---|---|
| Arbelour | Pernod Ricard |
| Allt á Bhainne (Chivas) | Pernod Ricard |
| Ardmore (Teachers) | Pernod Ricard |
| Auchroisk | Diageo |
| Aultmore (Dewars) | Bacardi |
| Balmenach | Inverhouse |
| Benriach (Chivas) | Intra Trading SA |
| Benrinnes | Diageo |
| Benromach | Gordon & McPhail |
| Caperdonich (Chivas) | Pernod Ricard |
| Cardhu (Johnny Walker Red) | Diageo |
| Cragganmore (White Horse) | Diageo |
| Craigellachie (White Horse) | Bacardi |
| Dailuaine (Johnny Walker) | Diageo |
| Dalwhinnie | Diageo |
| Glen Elgin | Diageo |
| Glen Grant | Pernod Ricard |
| Glen Keith | Pernod Ricard |
| Glen Moray | LVMH |
| Glen Spray | Diageo |
| Glenburgie (Ballantines) | Pernod Ricard |
| Glendronach (Teachers) | Pernod Ricard |
| Glendullan | Diageo |
| Glenfarclas | J&G Grant |
| Glenfiddich | William Grant |
| Glenlivet (Chivas) | Pernod Ricard |
| Glenlossie | Diageo |
| Glenrothes | Edrington Group |
| Glentauchers | Pernod Ricard |
| Inchgower | Diageo |

| | |
|---|---|
| Knockando (J & B) | Diageo |
| Knockdhu | Inver House |
| Linkwood (Bells, White Horse) | Diageo |
| Longmorn | Pernod Ricard |
| MacDuff | Bacardi |
| Mannochmore (Haigh) | Bacardi |
| Miltonduff (Ballantines) | Pernod Ricard |
| Mortlach | Diageo |
| Royal Brackla | Bacardi |
| Speyburn | Inver House |
| Strathisla Chivas | Pernod Ricard |
| Strathmill | Diageo |
| Tamdhu (Famous Grouse) | Edrington Group |
| The Balvenie | William Grant & Son |
| The Macallan (Cutty Sark) | Edrington Group |
| Tomatin | Takara,Shuzo,Okura |
| Tomintoul | Angus Dundee |
| Tormore (Ballantines) | Pernod Ricard |

## THE EASTERN HIGHLANDS

| | |
|---|---|
| Fettercain | Whyte & Mackay |
| Glen Garioch | Suntory |
| Glencadam (Ballentines) | Angus Dundee |
| Royal Lochnagar | Diageo |

## THE NORTHERN HIGHLANDS

| | |
|---|---|
| Balblair | Inver House |
| Clynelish & Brora | Diageo |
| Dalmore | Whyte & Mackay |
| Glen Ord (Dewars) | Diageo |
| Glenmorangie | LVMH |
| Old Pulteney | Inver House |
| Teaninich | Diageo |

# THE MIDLANDS
# (CENTRAL HIGHLANDS)

| | |
|---|---|
| Aberfeldy (Dewars & JW Red) | Bacardi |
| Blair Atholl | Diageo |
| Deanston | CL World Brands |
| Edradour | Signatory Vintage |
| Glenturret | Edrington Group |
| Tullibardine | Tullibardine |

## THE WESTERN HIGHLANDS

| | |
|---|---|
| Ben Nevis | The Nikka Distilling |
| Loch Lomond | Loch Lomond |
| Oban (Bells) | Diageo |

## THE LOWLANDS

| | |
|---|---|
| Auchentoshan | Suntory |
| Bladnoch | R. Armstrong |
| Glengoyne | Ian McLeod |
| Glenkinchie (Haigh Gold) | Diageo |

## TABLE "E"

## DISTILLERY'S SINGLE MALT USED IN PRODUCTION OF BLENDS

These are just a few examples:

| Distillery | Percentage of production used for Single malts | Balance Used in Blends |
|---|---|---|
| Aberfeldy | 5% of production | 95% |
| Ardmore | 5% of production | 95% |
| Aultmore | Unknown % (very small) | NA |
| Benriach | Unknown % (very small) | NA |
| Bunnahabin | 5% of production | 95% |
| Caol la | Unknown % used for s. malts until 02 | NA |
| Cardhu | 30% of production | 60% |
| Cragganmore | 30% of production | 60% |
| Dalwhinnie | 10% of production | 90% |
| Fettarcain | 4% of production | 95% |
| Gelnfarclas | 50% of production | 50% |
| Glen Ord | 10% of production | 80% |
| Glendronach | 10% of production | 80% |
| Glenturrett | 70% of production | 30% |

## NEW DISTILLERIES

## BLACKWOOD

Blackwood distillery is located on the Shetland Islands. (See the Islands section for complete descriptions)

## GLENGYLE / KILKERRAN

The first 'Glengyle' distillery was built in 1872 or 1873 by William Mitchell. He built Glengyle after a quarrel with his brother, John, prompted him to leave Springbank. The Campbeltown distillery operated for half a century until it was finally closed in 1925. The production buildings at Glengyle were pretty much restored by the end of 2002. During the first half of 2003 the buildings were fitted with a mash tun, stills and a spent grains removal system. The first 'whisky' (Kilkerran) won't be bottled until 2007.

## KILCHOMAN

On the west coast of Islay at Rockside near Machair Bay, farmer Mark French has teamed up with entrepreneur Anthony Wills to establish Kilchoman Farm Distillery. Uniquely self sufficient, Kilchoman is a modern recreation of the farmhouse distilleries that are the basis of today's industry. Floor maltings have been built and the whole production process through to maturation and bottling will be undertaken on site. Initial production will be in the region of 80,000 bottles.

## DAFTMILL

A second new and little known farmhouse distillery is ready for commissioning in Fife. The Cuthbert family has built a small distillery in their farmyard in central Fife. Of a similar size to Kilchoman, Daftmill will initially not be malting on site and it is expected to produce a Lowland style and will become the third 'surviving' Lowland distillery. The owners are keen to point out that the Daftmill project should not be confused with the other proposed Fife distillery, Ladybank, of which no progress is known.

## LADYBANK

Members can invest in the distillery and reserve their own stock. "The Club intends, by focusing on very small production quantities, to create one of the world's greatest single malt whiskies. By reducing yields so that we can always improve quality, and by distributing our whisky only to members and special guests who visit the distillery, Ladybank will add a new dimension to the world of Scotch Malt Whisky production."

## KININVIE

Kininvie has been an 'active' distillery since 1990. The owners of the distillery (WM Grant & Sons) are focusing their marketing efforts on their two main malt brands: Glenfiddich and Balvenie. They need the Kininvie malt whisky for their Grant's blends, but they don't seem overly eager to invest heavily in a third malt whisky brand.

## NORFOLK WHISKY COMPANY

The Norfolk development will be the first outside the Celtic fringes. The site was chosen partly because it is near a source of pure water and partly because of the ease with which tourists can reach it. No name has yet been chosen for the whisky.

## CORNISH CYDER FARM

The most recent Celtic nation to get its own malt whisky is Cornwall, (a joint venture between St Austell brewery and the Cornish Cyder Farm). It appears that whisky has not been distilled on Cornish soil until the 21st century and we look forward to tasting the first ever Cornish whisky in due course.

## THE WELSH WHISKY COMPANY

September 14th, 2000 something happened in Wales for the first time in over a century – they distilled whisky! This new company is producing a pot still whisky called Penderyn and the facility lies within a National Park that has an abundance of pure underground water. They are producing a unique malt whisky with a light easy drinking style.

## Chapter 17

# Glossary

*Abv:* Alcohol by volume. The strength of an alcohol or spirit measured as the percentage of pure alcohol contained in the liquid. For instance, a whisky of 40% Abv will contain 40% of pure alcohol, the rest being made up of water, mainly, plus various congeners.

*Age:* The minimum age for a whisky in Scotland and Ireland is 3 years old. The age stated on a whisky bottle is that of the youngest whisky in the vatting. Once bottled, a whisky does not mature any more.

*Age Statement:* This gives the age of the "youngest" component of the whisky. Note that maturation stops at bottling so both the year and the age may be significant. A 12 Year Old whisky bottled 4 years ago is still a 12 Year Old, not a 16 year old, though different years occasionally may be quoted.

*Aledhydes:* Grassy, leathery aromas.

*Angel Share:* The name given to the alcohol which evaporates from the casks during the maturation – amounting to approximately 2% per year of the cask's content.

*Aquavitae:* Latin for "water of life" from which the Gaelic "uisge beatha" and "usquebaugh" were derived. The modern "whisky" is just a derivative of "usque."

*Barley:* The only cereal grain used to produce malt whisky.

*Barrel:* A term refering to a cask in general. Barrel is also often used to refer specifically to the traditional American type of cask with a capacity of about 180 litres. (200 litre Bourbon cask)

*Bastard Malt:* Whisky of dubious origins.

*Blend or Blended Whisky:* This is whisky that contains both malt and grain whisky in varying proportions and ages from a variety of distilleries.

*Blending:* The mixing of "straight" whiskies (malt, bourbon or rye) with grain whisky in proportions determined by a whisky blender who is attempting to achieve a particular style of whisky or consistency of character across a number of years.

*Body:* Mouth feel of a whisky.

*Bourbon:* U.S. Whiskey (note the "e") that is produced from a mash of not less than 51% corn grain distilled to a maximum 80% Abv (160° American proof) and put into charred, new oak barrels at a strength of no more than 62.5% Abv. Bourbon casks are charcoaled on the inside before use to impart flavour to the maturing spirit.

*Brewing:* The process of mashing grain in hot water then fermenting the result with yeast to produce beer or wash.

*Burnt Ale:* Also called Pot Ale. The liquor left in the Low Wines or Wash Still after the first distillation. It is either discharged as waste or converted to animal feed.

*Butt:* A type of cask currently used for the maturation of Scotch whisky or Irish whiskey, with a capacity of approximately 500 litres.

*Caramel:* A dark brown substance made from sugar. It is added to some whisky as a colouring agent.

*Cask Strength:* Whisky bottled at, or near to, the strength it comes out of the cask. This depends upon age and can vary considerably, distillery to distillery, age to age.

*Casks:* Once distilled, whisky is left to mature in specialized barrels called *casks;* usually these casks previously contained sherry or bourbon, but more exotic casks such as port, cognac, calvados, and Bordeaux wine are sometimes used. (Irish Whiskies are also aged in used Sherry barrels, but without the charring characteristic of aging Scotch Whisky.) Bourbon production is a nearly inexhaustible generator of used barrels, due to a regulation requiring the use of new North American white oak barrels.

*Charcoal mellowing:* Used for Tennessee whiskey. The new spirit is filtered through charcoal before going into the cask. Some may be filtered through charcoal again after cask aging and before bottling.

*Charring:* Or "burning" of the inside of the cask. The insides of new oak casks are exposed to flame, charring them, which adds colour and a smoky flavour to the resulting spirit.

*Chillfiltration:* The elimination of some congeners by the filtration of whisky which has been previously chilled to a temperature more or less close to $0^{\circ C}$. It improves the clarity and prevents hazing at low temperatures (which has strictly no consequence) at the price of the loss of some aromatic components.

*Coffey Still:* Also called Patent or Column Still. A type of still working through a continuous process. It is composed of an analyzing column and of a rectifying column and is generally used for the production of grain whisky.

*Congeners:* Chemical compounds produced during fermentation and maturation. These congeners include esters, acids, aldehydes and higher alcohols. They are impurities, but they give whisky its flavour.

*Continuous Distillation:* The distillation of grain whisky in a patent still which works on a continuous process, as opposed to distillation in a pot still which is a batch process. The cheaper and faster alternative to the pot still.

*Cooper:* A distillery worker who is responsible for the assembly and maintenance of the casks. In the nineteenth century he was probably the highest paid man at the distillery.

*Corn Whiskey:* (US term) A whiskey made from a mash containing at least 80% corn and, if it is aged at all, must be done so in used or uncharred oak barrels.

*Cut:* The critical moment when the stillman will stop collecting the Middle Cut, which is the only fraction kept to become whisky. The alcohol distilled after the cut is known as tails. The cut is the middle portion of the spirit coming off the spirit still. The cut is the best part of the distillate, and is saved and put into barrel. The foreshots and feints are re distilled.

*Demineralised Water:* The fifth use of water in the production process. This is used to reduce the strength of whisky prior to bottling.

*Distillation:* The separation of alcohol and water as being achieved in a still. The vaporization of an alcoholic liquid by heat, followed by the collection by condensation of its alcohol content. Distillation does not create any alcohol; alcohol is produced only during fermentation.

*Double maturation:* Is said of a whisky having benefited from a finishing, or second maturation, in a second cask of different origin and characteristics.

*Doublings:* The spirit produced by a secondary distillation. Often referred to as high wines (but in US, confusingly, high wines are the product of the first distillation).

*Draff:* The solid particles lying in the mashtun after the wort has been drawn off. Draff is a much sought after food for cattle.

*Dram:* In Gaelic, a measurement of whisky.

*Dunnage:* The traditional means of racking casks in a bonded warehouse.

*Enzymes:* Complex chemical compounds which help to break down the starch within the endosperm into sugars during germination.

*Esters:* Fruity, flowery aromas.

*Ethanol:* The primary alcohol produced during the fermentation of the yeast.

*Feints:* Also known as the tail of the distillation, tails or aftershots. The last cut of the output from the low wines or spirit still. This liquid is returned back to the low wines and feints charger for re distillation as part of the next batch.

*Fermentation:* The transformation of sugar contained in the wash under the action of yeast, producing alcohol and carbon dioxide with an emission of heat.

*Finishing:* After its initial maturation is carried out in the traditional manner (usually in a former bourbon cask), a whisky is finished when it is transferred to a cask of different origin and characteristics to benefit from a further maturation. Finishing will produce a double maturation whisky which will bring enhanced complexity in nosing and tasting and may provide a new balance to the whisky.

*First Fill:* Refers to casks that are being filled with whisky for the first time, even though they may have already been used for bourbon or sherry.

*Floor Maltings:* The floor maltings consist of one or more floors of the malt house where barley is spread on the stone floor(s) after steeping and is then allowed to germinate under controlled conditions.

*Foreshots:* The first fraction of the second distillation preceding the middle cut. The foreshots are not kept for the whisky. As the first spirit to come off the spirit still, the foreshots are high in alcohol (75–80% Abv), contain too many volatile compounds, and are re distilled.

*Germination:* The process that takes place in the floor maltings in which the steeped barley is spread on the floor (the barley is now known as the piece) and allowed to sprout, forming shoots and rootlets, and is left there for about seven days. It is tended regularly to keep the temperature constant at about 16°C. At seven days the barley is now known as green malt and further growth is prevented by the barley being dried in the kiln.

*Grain:* The seeds of a cereal crop such as maize, corn, rye, wheat and barley.

*Grain whisky:* Whisky that is produced by the patent or continuous still. The mash consists of a proportion of malted barley together with unmalted cereals such as wheat or maize.

*Grist:* Crushed malt, looking like a kind of flour, which will be mixed with hot water in the mashtun to produce the wort.

*High Wines:* The product of the first distillation in a batch or pot still process. The high wines are distilled for a second time in the spirit still, or doubler.

*Hogshead:* Traditional Scottish cask, generally of rather squat proportion and whose capacity, which somewhat varies according to the area, is usually about 250 litres.

*Hydrometer:* A floating device usually made of glass, which gives an indication via a scale on its side of the specific gravity of a liquid in which it is floating. The scale is read at the water/air boundary of the liquid being measured.

*IB:* Independent bottler.

*Irish Malt Whiskey:* (note the "e") is produced in exactly the same way as Scotch malt whisky with the exception that the majority is triple distilled.

*Irish whiskey:* A spirit obtained by distillation from a mash of cereal grains saccharified by the diastase of malt. By law, it cannot be called Irish whiskey unless it has been distilled in Ireland and has matured in an oak cask in Ireland for at least three years.

*Kiln:* The kiln is used to dry the green malt which kills the germ of the growing grain, once germination to the required degree has been achieved.

*Lincoln County Process:* Another name for charcoal mellowing.

*Liquor:* Name given to the hot water mixed with the grist in the mashtun during the mashing process.

*Lomond still:* Peculiar column shaped still with a refluxing coil in its head which enables the still to be "tuned" to produce a lighter or heavier spirit. This allows a distillery to produce two distinctly different malts from the same set of stills. It works on the same principle as a normal pot still.

*Low wines:* The alcohol produced during the first distillation, with a strength of approximately 25% Abv. The spirit to come off the wash still. Its strength is usually about 21% Abv.

*Malt:* Barley after its starch has been transformed into fermentable sugars. Any grain which has been made to germinate, and then been dried to arrest growth.

*Malt Grist:* Milled malted barley, sometimes just known as grist. The malt grist hopper is used to store freshly milled malt grist until required for mashing with hot water in the mash tun.

*Malted Barley:* Sometimes known as just malt, malted barley is the grains of barley, softened in water in the steep, allowed to germinate on the floor maltings and dried in the kiln to stop the germination process. If the kiln is laced with peat, then a peaty aroma is imparted to the malted barley. The malting process converts the stored starch into soluble compounds, such as the sugar maltose, and by doing so makes fermentation possible.

*Malting:* The process through which barley is transformed into malt, by artificially starting up its germination process, which will be eventually stopped at the kilning stage. It is the controlled germination of grain.

*Malt Whisky:* Whisky which has been produced exclusively from the distillation of a wort of malt, usually in pot stills. Whisky made purely from malted barley.

*Marrying:* Occasionally bottlings are produced from one single cask – the so-called 'single single' malts. More normally, several casks of similar ages from the one distillery will be 'married' by vatting them together then maturing them for a further few months.

*Mash:* The product of mixing grist with hot water in the mashtun. The mash will eventually become wort when it is drawn off at the end of the process.

*Mashing:* The process during which the wort is produced. It involves mixing the grist with hot water in order to dissolve the fermentable sugars.

*Mashing Machine:* A device intended to ensure the correct mixing of grist with hot water when they are poured into the mashtun.

*Maturation: Or aging. The process through which the whisky contained in its cask acquires its character.*

*Middle Cut:* Also known as the heart of the distillation. The second cut of the output from the low wines or spirit still, mainly containing pure alcohol. This is the "raison d'être" for the distillation process. This raw spirit is diverted to the spirit receiver and eventually into casks for maturation into single malt Scotch whisky.

*NAS:* No Age Statement.

*Nose:* The characteristic aroma of a particular whisky.

*Nosing:* A method of sampling whisky by sense of smell only. Used by professional tasters and blenders to avoid fatiguing the palate and/or intoxication.

*OB:* Official / Owner Bottling (er)

*Oak:* The traditional timber from which casks are made. Bourbon casks are made from American white oak, sherry butts from European oak.

*Organic Whisky:* Following the current popular trends in food and drink, this is whisky made from barley grown in ground that is free from inorganic fertilizers and treated with non–chemical pesticides.

*PPM:* Phenols per million.

*Pagoda (Roof):* Characteristic style of roof found on a traditional distillery kiln. Roughly pyramidal and surmounted by a square chimney or vent with its own pyramid shaped cover. The chimney or vent often contains a fan which draws the smoke up through the malt.

*Peat:* Organic compound resulting from the partial decomposing of plants. Smoke produced during its combustion at the kilning stage allows the production of peated malt, which is used to produce whiskies of a particularly powerful character. These originate generally on the island of Islay and are held in a high reputation.

*Peat Fire:* Usually some or all of the heat used in the kiln comes from the burning of dried peat in the kiln's fire. This creates the peat reek that helps to flavour the more peated malted barleys.

*Peat Reek:* The smoky flavour imparted to the malt during its time in the kiln due to peat smoke condensate settling on the grain and increasing its phenol content.

*Peated Malt:* Malt whisky with the smoky smell that comes from treating barley with peat.

*Phenol:* Chemical compounds acquired by malt from peat during the kilning process. It is responsible for the peaty flavour of Islay whiskies in particular. Peaty, smoky aromas.

*Pot Still:* Device used for the batch distillation process. It is a large, copper kettle filled with wash which is then heated. Alcohol, being more volatile than water, evaporates first before being condensed. The first distillation produces the low wines, with a strength of about 25% Abv, which are then distilled a second time to produce the spirit, collected at about 70% Abv. In pot still distillation the liquid is usually distilled twice, occasionally three times, first in a wash still and then in a spirit still.

*Proof:* Originally meaning "of tried strength or quality," "proof" acquired new meaning with the invention of the hydrometer – a floating instrument used to determine the specific gravity of a fluid, in this case an alcohol/water mixture.

*Puncheon:* A cask of equal capacity to a butt, or a 450 litre sherry cask.

*Pure Malt:* Whisky made only from malted barley that has not been blended with anything else. It may be the product of just one distillery (if more, usually called a single malt) or it may be a mixture of malt whiskies from more than one distillery (if more, usually called a vatted malt). Any age statement refers to the youngest component whisky.

*Racking:* Transferring spirit into casks from another container, for instance, a damaged cask or a tanker.

*Red Layer:* (US term) A layer of caramelized wood sugars that is formed when the barrels are 'toasted' and charred.

*Refill:* Refers to casks that have already been used at least once for whisky maturation (first fill) and are being pressed into service again. Second fill and third fill are not uncommon.

*Rye whiskey:* Whiskey made from at least 51% rye. Production is similar to that of bourbon.

*SMSW:* Single Malt Scotch Whisky.

*SWA:* Scotch Whisky Association.

*Scotch:* A spirit obtained by distillation from a mash of cereal grains that have been saccharified by the diastase of malt. By law, it cannot be called "Scotch whisky" unless it has been distilled in Scotland and has matured in an oak cask in Scotland for at least three years.

*Scotch on the rocks:* Malt whisky is drunk either as a neat spirit or with a small quantity of water to taste. It should *never* be drunk with soda or other mixers, neither should it be necessary to drink it "on the rocks."

*Scotch whisky:* Whisky distilled and aged in Scotland for a minimum of 3 years.

*Single Cask:* Sometimes called a Single– Single Malt (as in single distillery, single cask), it is malt whisky taken from one individual cask and is the product of just one distillation run from just one distillery. It is usually sold at cask strength (around 55% Abv–65% Abv depending upon the particular distillery) and the process of chillfiltration is frequently omitted. The information on the label is usually extended to include the cask number, date of distillation, date of bottling and the number of bottles produced from that cask. It may also be authenticated by the signature of one of the distillery's managers.

*Single grain whisky:* Grain whisky made at just one distillery that has not been mixed with any whisky from elsewhere. However, the whisky may come from many different casks of varying ages. Any age statement on the bottle refers to the youngest component whisky.

*Single malt whisky:* Malt whisky made at just one distillery. However, the whisky may come from many different casks of varying ages. Any age statement on the bottle refers to the youngest component whisky.

*Sour Mash Process:* Approximately 25% of the mash from the previous batch is held back and added to the next batch. This contains some of the yeast needed for fermentation, helps to keep out wild yeast and ensures a consistency between different batches. This is known as the 'Sour Mash' process and is the normal method of production in all straight whiskies, though only a few state this on the label.

*Spirit:* The middle cut collected from the spirit still on the second distillation with a strength of about 70% Abv. It is only after this cut has matured in cask for a minimum of three years that it becomes whisky.

*Spirit Receiver:* A collecting vessel used to collect the wanted output of the spirit still(s) (the middle cut) prior to it being passed into the spirit filling vat.

*Spirit Safe:* A large, usually highly polished, brass box that is divided into 2 chambers (or 3 in the case of triple distillation) with a brass bound glass door at the front secured by a stout brass bar with large padlocks at either end.

*Spirit Still:* Pot still used for the second distillation and in which the low wines are transformed into spirit. In pot still distillation, the second (occasionally third) still of the process.

*Staves:* Longitudinal pieces of wood which are assembled for making the body of the cask.

*Steam Coil:* A steam coil is a coiled copper pipe in the bottom of a wash still (most usually) through which steam is passed in order to heat the liquid contents of the still.

*Steam Heater:* Stills are onion shaped, made from copper, and are usually heated internally by a steam heater, a coil of tubing that conveys steam.

*Straight Whiskey:* Whiskey with no colouring or flavouring added.

*Sugar:* An energy source from which alcohol and carbon dioxide can be produced by the action of enzymes. A member of the carbohydrate family.

*Tails:* The last fraction of the second distillation, following the middle cut, which is not kept for whisky.

*Tennessee whiskey:* As bourbon, but filtered through a minimum of ten feet of sugar maple charcoal. This is not a legal requirement, but is the method by which Tennessee whiskies are currently produced.

Triple Distillation: Traditionally a Lowland method, triple distillation simply adds another stage of distillation to the normal double distillation process common throughout Scotland. Only Springbank, Auchentoshan and Rosebank still employ the technique while Talisker stopped it in 1926. Most Irish malt whiskey is produced by triple distillation.

*Tun Room:* A double decker room in which the washbacks are situated. The lower ground floor part is kept locked during the fermentation process for safety reasons. The washbacks stand on the ground floor and project up into the first floor area. The fermentation process is controlled by the "tun room man."

*Unpeated Malt:* Malt whisky made from barley which has been kiln dried without peat.

*Vatted Grain:* A term rarely found these days. Vatted grain is whisky produced by mixing together two or more grain whiskies (usually up to a maximum of six) from two or more different distilleries. The vatting of a mixture of grain whiskies from the same distillery but at different ages is more usually called single grain. Any age statement refers to the youngest component whisky.

*Vatted Malt:* Vatted malt whisky is produced by mixing together two or more malt whiskies (usually up to a maximum of six) from two or more different distilleries. Originally the term applied as well to a mixture of malt whiskies from the same distillery but at different ages – this is more usually called single malt. Any age statement refers to the youngest component whisky.

*Vatting:* The mixing of whiskies. Vatting is usually taken as meaning that only malt or only grain whiskies are contained in the mixture. If both types of whiskies were to be included, the process would be blending.

*WIP:* Unbottled whisky.

*Wash:* The low strength beer product of fermentation in the washback which is used in the wash still for the first stage of distillation. Typically, the wash is at about 8% Abv. Sometimes known as the brew or, in the US, beer.

*Wash Still:* The wash still (also known as beer still) is the still in which the first stage of distillation takes place, the retained output of which, containing almost pure alcohol, is used as the input to the second stage of distillation in the low wines or spirit still for double distillation or the intermediate still for triple distillation. The unretained output, containing almost pure water, is sent to waste. The first chamber of the spirit safe is used to direct the flow to the appropriate destination.

*Whiskey:* Different spelling of "whisky," usually associated to products from Ireland or the USA.

*Whisky:* A spirit obtained from the distillation of a mash of cereals at a strength lower than 94.8%, matured for a minimum of 3 years in an oak cask whose capacity should not exceed 700 litres and is bottled at a strength of not less than 40% Abv.

Worm: Coiled copper pipe, immersed in cold running water in a worm tub, in which the vapour given off from the stills is condensed back into liquid.

*Wort:* A sweet liquid resulting from the mixing of grist with hot water once it has been drawn off the mashtun. It will become wash after it is fermented. The liquid, high in fermentable starches, is drained off the mashtun and enters the washback for fermentation.

*Yeast:* Unicellular fungus responsible for the fermentation process, which lives on sugar and multiplies by producing alcohol and carbon dioxide.

*YO:* "Year old," as in 10 Year Old whisky.

Many thanks to the following websites and individuals for their outstanding photographs and clipart.

| | |
|---|---|
| Page 1 – David & Goliath | www.kids.christianpost.com |
| Page 8 – Loch Dee Geese | www.gla.ac.uk |
| Page 23 – Isle of Arran Distillery | Michael Gill |
| Page 26 – Fields of Barley | www.hops.co.uk |
| Page 31 – Harvesting Peat for drying | www.freepages.books.com |
| Page 33 – Peat Bogs – a Natural Wetland | www.en.wikpedia.org |
| Page 36 – Pot Still | unknown |
| Page 43 – Connemara | www.cooleywhiskey.com |
| Page 44 – Tennessee Whisky Label | unknown |
| Page 48 – Casks | www.bruichladdich.com |
| Page 54 – Whisky Warehouses | www.fiona.gopherit.org |
| Page 57 – Cask Strength bottles | www.gordonandmacphail.com |
| Page 63 – Labels | www.thewhiskyexchange.com |
| Page 64 – Old Malt Cask Labels | www.douglaslaing.com |
| Page 68 – Bottles & Glasses | unknown |
| Page 74 – Cheese Heads | www.patsaunderswhite.com |
| Page 75 – Whisky & Cheese | Michael Gill |
| Page 85 – Bowmore Distillery | www.armin-grewe.com |
| Page 87 – Bruichladdich Distillery | www.scotlandview.co.uk |
| Page 89 – Laphroaig Distillery | www.travellerspoint.com |
| Page 91 – Lagavulin Distillery | undiscoveredscotland.co.uk |
| Page 93 – Ardbeg Distillery | www.winepictures.com |
| Page 95 – Bunnahabhain Distillery | undiscoveredscotland.co.uk |
| Page 97 – Caol Ila Distillery | www.aflodal.com |
| Page 100 – Isle of Arran Distillery | www.arranwhisky.com |
| Page 104 – Isle of Jura Distillery | www.scottishholidays.net |
| Page 108 – Talisker Distillery | www.geograph.co.uk |
| Page 112 – Tobermory Distillery | www.scotlandwhisky.co |
| Page 116 – Highland Park | www.europeforvisitors.com |
| Page 118 – Scapa Distillery | www.awa.dk |
| Page 121 – Blackwood Distillery | www.geograph.co.uk |

## MAPS OF SCOTLAND:

The various Maps of Scotland were found on numerous tourist websites. Page 11-Isle of Skye; Page 15-Map of Scotland; Page 80-Scotland's Islands; Page 83–Map of Islay; Page 99 – Isle of Arran; Page 102- Isle of Jura; Page 106-Map-Isle of Skye; Page 110-Map Isle of Mull; Page 114- Map of the Orkneys & the Shetlands.

## TABLES:

## RECOMMENDED READING

- www.scotchwhisky.net
- en.wikpedia.org
- www.maltwhisky.com

## EXCELLENT SOURCE READING

- Whisky Magazine
- Malt Advocate

# Coming in 2007, "Whisky Today" updated.

- ☐ The latest industry news of 2006
- ☐ Much more cheese matching
- ☐ Food & whisky – Seven– course dinner suggestions
- ☐ More distillery profiles
- ☐ Casks continued

ISBN 141208328-1

9 781412 083287

Edwards Brothers Malloy
Oxnard, CA  USA
March 6, 2013